PUBLISHED TITLES

Rodney Barker *Politics, Peoples and Government*
C. J. Bartlett *British Foreign Policy in the Twentieth Century*
Jeremy Black *Robert Walpole and the Nature of Politics
in Early Eighteenth-Century Britain*
Anne Curry *The Hundred Years War*
John W. Derry *British Politics in the Age of Fox, Pitt and Liverpool*
William Gibson *Church, State and Society, 1760–1850*
Ann Hughes *The Causes of the English Civil War*
Ronald Hutton *The British Republic, 1649–1660*
Kevin Jefferys *The Labour Party since 1945*
D. M. Loades *The Mid-Tudor Crisis,1545–1565*
Diarmaid MacCulloch *The Later Reformation in England, 1547–1603*
Keith Perry *British Politics and the American Revolution*
A. J. Pollard *The Wars of the Roses*
David Powell *British Politics and the Labour Question, 1868–1990*
Michael Prestwich *English Politics in the Thirteenth Century*
Richard Rex *Henry VIII and the English Reformation*
G. R. Searle *The Liberal Party: Triumph and Disintegration, 1886–1929*
Paul Seaward *The Restoration, 1660–1668*
Robert Stewart *Party and Politics, 1830–1852*
John W. Young *Britain and European Unity, 1945–92*

History of Ireland

D. G. Boyce *The Irish Question and British Politics, 1868–1986*

History of Scotland

Keith M. Brown *Kingdom or Province? Scotland and the Regal Union,
1603–1715*

History of Wales

J. Gwynfor Jones *Early Modern Wales, c.1525–1640*

Please see overleaf for forthcoming titles

WITHDRAWN

FORTHCOMING TITLES

Please also note that a sister series, *Social History in Perspective*, is now available, covering the key topics in social, cultural and religious history.

POLITICS, PEOPLES AND GOVERNMENT

Themes in British Political Thought since the Nineteenth Century

RODNEY BARKER

M

St. Martin's Press

First published in Great Britain 1994 by
THE MACMILLAN PRESS LTD
Houndmills, Basingstoke, Hampshire RG21 2XS
and London
Companies and representatives
throughout the world

A catalogue record for this book is available
from the British Library.

ISBN 0–333–56344–1 hardcover
ISBN 0–333–56345–X paperback

Printed in Hong Kong

First published in the United States of America 1994 by
Scholarly and Reference Division,
ST. MARTIN'S PRESS, INC.,
175 Fifth Avenue,
New York, N.Y. 10010

ISBN 0–312–10382–4

Library of Congress Cataloging-in-Publication Data
Barker, Rodney.
Politics, peoples and government : themes in British political
thought since the nineteenth century / Rodney Barker.
p.   cm. — (British history in perspective)
Includes bibliographical references and index.
ISBN 0–312–10382–4 (St. Martin's Press)
1. Political science—Great Britain—History.   I. Title.
II. Series: British history in perspective (Houndmills, Basingstoke,
England)
JA84.G7B35   1994
320.5'0941—dc20   93–30828
                                                         CIP

For Tom

CONTENTS

1

POLITICAL THOUGHT IN BRITAIN

I International and Domestic

Conservatives, wrote F. J. C. Hearnshaw in 1933, often seem to distrust thinking and writing, and conservatism 'tends to be silent, lethargic, confused, incoherent, inarticulate, unimpressive'.[1] E. P. Thompson, writing almost half a century later and from a quite different point on the political spectrum, seemed to be saying something much the same about the British as a whole when he referred to 'a hostile national culture' which was 'both smug and resistant to intellectuality'.[2] But both writers went on to illustrate how wrong it was despite this to suppose that the British distrust theory. It is rather the case that they distrust certain kinds of theory. For the history of British politics is in part a history of a rich outpouring of speaking and writing of a speculative and argumentative kind about all those practical matters to which theory, unless it is to be a private game, must address itself.

This argumentative political thought has dealt with all aspects of the public and governmental life of the country and can range from F. A. Hayek recommending the spontaneity of markets to T. S. Eliot calling for an intellectual and spiritual elite, from George Orwell talking about socialism as fraternity, to Quintin Hogg praising the lack of interest which true conservatives have in any kind of politics at all.

But if it is true that Britain has not been doggedly anti-

1

theoretical, and so has not differed either from continental Europe or from the rest of the world in the scope of its political thought, is perhaps the opposite true? Many of the issues which have been raised in political argument in this country – the rights of women, the nature of citizenship, the proper economic responsibilities of government, or the function of property – seem to be international or universal, rather than particularly British. What is there that is distinctively British at all? Political thought in Britain, like that anywhere else, may have had its own particular character. But it has shared contexts and problems with political thought in other modern and European countries: the replacement of an agrarian society based on relatively small scale and direct agricultural production by an urban society where livings were made principally in money, in large productive units or large organisations; the growth of government and of the organisation of public life by bureaucracy and management; the massive extension of the powers and responsibilities of the state; the rise of democracy.

But there are unique features as well: not a theme or a principle, but a historical conjuncture. There may be many elements which Britain has had in common with much of the rest of the world, but the relative emphasis and the overall pattern of those elements have still been distinctive. The history of Britain, of which political thought has been a part, cannot simply be reduced to a local example of general themes. One side of this particular, British, history has certainly been a local response to particular versions of developments common to all modern societies: industrialisation, urbanisation, the development, and decline, of an industrial, class society. At the same time specifically British thought was possible because there existed specifically British circumstances with which such thought could be concerned. The development of an urban society in Britain was both like and unlike similar developments in France or Germany, just as London or Glasgow were like, and unlike, Munich or Lyons.

So there are two dimensions to the history of political thought in Britain. The first dimension is the response to developments of modern society which, though they were international, were often treated as if they were specific to Britain: the growth of a commercial society, the extension of the franchise, and the extended powers of the modern state. The second dimension has been a British response to events which despite their particularity are seen, because they take place abroad, as of universal significance. Foreign wars and revolutions have often had as great an effect on the general terms of political argument as have events within Britain. The First and Second World Wars affected the acceptable limits of state action; the revolutions in Russia in 1917 or in 1989 affected the ways people thought about the purposes and nature of government. So a part of the context of political thought in Britain is the varying influence of argument from North America or Europe, or of events taking place beyond the British Isles. This had always been so. The French Revolution of 1789 or the rise of European nationalisms in the nineteenth century were early examples of the fascination which wars and revolutions viewed through the simplifying lenses of distance could exercise. Russia, Germany, Italy and Spain were to exert a similar fascination in the twentieth century, and by its second half wars in South East Asia and revolutions in eastern Europe were to have as important a place in the development of the political imagination and demonology as the Russian Revolution or the Spanish Civil War had in the first half.

Domestic instances of universal phenomena, and external events of symbolic import, have thus intermingled as the context within which political thought developed. The French Revolution appeared to both friends and enemies as a potential catalyst for radical movements within Britain; unrest on the Clyde after the First World War seemed to draw both on domestic industrial discontents and on the revolutionary example of the Bolshevik Revolution of 1917. The mundane expansion of domestic possibilities could intertwine powerfully with the spectacular revelation of foreign ones. When at the end of the Second World War F. A. Hayek published *The Road to Serfdom*, the ultimate horror with which he frightened his readers was totalitarianism in Germany and Russia. But the fear which prompted the author himself and which he presented as the first step towards the apocalypse was the less spectacular but more immediate possibility of social democracy and collectivist economic planning in Britain.

II Political Thought in Historical Context

Political thought since the end of the eighteenth century has passed through four broad historical periods which have displayed changes in the relative importance of the domestic and the international dimensions. These periods are not hermetically sealed, and there are continuations of one phase long after its predominance has ceased. During the first period England – and it is appropriate to speak of England rather than of Britain – could be viewed as self-sufficient with its own political thought. Problems, whilst they might be of general human consequence, and considered in the light of writers other than British, were not seen to depend on events beyond these shores. The self-containment of this period was shattered by the French Revolution and by the rise of domestic democracy. But whilst this was a feature of eighteenth century Britain, the view that both our problems and our solutions, although not unique, may nonetheless be particular is a persistent one. When E. P. Thompson declared in 1973, defending British, even English, traditions against continental high theory, that 'English intellectuals have played the role of jesters to the universal priests (Catholic or Anti-Catholic) of Western Europe', he was working within a mode with which both Cobbett in the nineteenth century and Orwell in the twentieth would have felt some affinities.[3]

In the second period England – and it is still England as much as Britain – was becoming aware of its increasing international power, and its political thought, whilst conducted as an English affair, nonetheless was seen as something which might have lessons for other, less enlightened, parts of the globe. At the same time the development of democracy, of towns, of industry, and of visible poverty raised new questions both of public action and responsibility and of the right to participate in politics. In the nineteenth century it had been supposed, by anti-imperialists and free traders more than by their opponents, that 'Britain's destiny was to serve the universal interests of mankind',[4] and these assumptions continued on into the different arguments of the twentieth century. The influence of the imperial epoch long outlasted the empire itself. In the second half of the twentieth century, James Hinton was still able to talk of 'imperialist pacifism', a form of argument which assumed that the eyes of the world were on Britain, and that the principal consequence of any political initiative here was the lessons it gave to the rest of the globe.[5]

In the third period, Britain became a participant in great events which had their origins elsewhere, whether it were international proletarian revolution or the international defence of property. The consumption or employment of ideas and aspirations from overseas was accentuated by the decline of Britain as a world power. When a commanding position in Europe was combined with a command of empire across and around the world, Britain could appear to itself as the source rather than destination of political thought, exporting liberalism, progressivism, or constitutionalism in intellectual free trade or free benefaction. A decline in the military, diplomatic and economic stature of Britain did not lead simply or ineluctably to a decline in intellectual creativity or supposed intellectual dominance. But it accompanied it and was matched appropriately by it. When Britain became a major recipient of external influences, this could mean either attraction or revulsion. The enthusiasm generated by revolutions in Russia, Germany, Italy and Spain between the two world wars was countered by the aversion to over-ambitious politics when the domestic record of Bolshevism and Nazism came to be more widely acknowledged after 1945. The Cold War, mobilising national sentiment and political and economic conservatism in the same cause, had a greater impact on political thought than the real war of 1939–45 which preceded it.

The fourth and final period saw the dissolution of intellectual frontiers and the creation of an international intellectual community, or at least of an intellectual multinational. By the last decade of the century a complete cycle seemed to have been achieved. The Russian Revolution of 1917 may have mesmerised both radicals and conservatives for half a century. But glasnost and perestroika, and the upsurge of democratic nationalisms in eastern Europe, swept away both the threat and the hope, and in the year that marked the 200th anniversary of the French Revolution, that great outburst of intellectual enthusiasms was re-established as the starting point for both growth and reaction in European and British political thought. Liberty, equality and fraternity became once more the leading shibboleths of politics.

As important as the internationalisation of politics and the declining status and power of the United Kingdom, was the increasing ease of international communication by the written word. Without necessarily losing its specificity, British thought took place in an increasingly international context. And the less there is a specific sovereign British state whose activities encompass all that is of relevance to the public life of the inhabitants of these islands, the less will there be a corresponding distinctiveness of political thought. A dispersal of government leads to a dispersal of politics, of which political thought is an essential part. The further this development goes, the less likely is it that political thought written or read in the United Kingdom will relate specifically or exclusively to that country, or be explicable or locatable in terms of it. A prominent feminist political theorist such as Carole Pateman can begin in Britain, work first in Australia and then in the United States, and be read in all three. Similarly, the debate over markets in the last quarter of the twentieth century has been transnational rather than simply British.

By the last decade of the twentieth century, political argument is in Britain, rather than specifically British. Two instances illustrate this: the Salman Rushdie affair, and the formation of 'Charter 88'. Both were inexplicable in simply British terms. The first involved an appeal to an international Islamic community and its values. Not since the seventeenth century had religious faith involved political loyalties to persons or institutions abroad. Then, 'ultramontanism' had placed on Roman Catholic subjects of English monarchs the contrary claim of loyalty to the Papacy. Now the 'fatwah' or death sentence pronounced on the author Salman Rushdie by religious leaders in Iran seemed to make a similar claim on the allegiance of Muslims in the United Kingdom. The demands of the organisation 'Charter 88' for constitutional reform and a bill of rights specifically invoked the example of the Czechoslovak civil rights movement, 'Charter 77'. The implication was that citizens needed rights and safeguards irrespective of the economic colour of their regimes, and that just as the application of this principle was universal, so was its source and its expression international.

Membership of the European Community, and potential or actual conflict between its laws governing civil and political liberties and those of the United Kingdom have led to a greater awareness of the state at precisely the time when the concept is becoming less adequate or appropriate for describing the government of the people of the British Isles. But growing involvement with Europe has not been the only factor here. Up until 1989 discussion of the quality of political regimes had been inextricably bound up with the assessment of the policies, in particular the economic policies, which those regimes were following. In an ironic mirror image of Marx's assertion that states were to be understood in the light of the economic systems which they maintained, critics of eastern European state socialism took a willingness to interfere in the free operations of the market as infallible evidence not only of socialist intentions, but of despotic ones. It had been the argument of liberals like Hayek since the end of the Second World War that such an inference was unavoidable. The confusion of regimes, nationhoods and policies into which Europe was cast after 1989 facilitated a political assessment of forms of government which did not depend upon, or lead automatically to, a judgment on economic or social policies.

The internationalisation of political thought has been countered by the continuation of particular, national, characteristics. Both feminism and socialism retained elements which, whilst they might link them to particular arguments in other countries, marked them off from any single international or transnational, homogenised debate. Feminism in the United Kingdom, as in Europe as a whole, has been more heavily political than feminism in the United States, less psychologistic than feminism in

7

France. The revisions of socialism which had come by the end of the 1980s to be termed 'market socialism' were a particularly British phenomenon. The sources and points of reference are international or at least Atlantic, but the historical possibilities are British – certainly they have been located neither in the US nor, before 1989, in the USSR.

III Political Thought in Democratic Politics

Political thought as politics

Politics, in the direct democracy of classical Greece, was conducted by means of the spoken word. To involve yourself in politics was to speak, and to listen, to try to persuade and to be open in principle to persuasion. Speech and argument in the public assembly were the method by which views on the conduct and aims of public life were expressed and developed. In a modern representative democracy, distance and numbers ensure that writing takes the place of talking as the language of extended public discussion. No politician can hope to communicate with those whose support she seeks to cultivate or hopes to gain principally through direct speech. The public meeting might reach small numbers for relatively long periods of time, and radio and television larger numbers for shorter spans of attention. But the most important successor to the public debate of direct democracies is the private reading of public statements, arguments, comments and reports.

Writing and reading have not directly replaced verbal debate. The process has become more complicated and less homogeneous. There are varieties of audience and 'producers', and varieties of communication. But political thought, in a sense in which it would have been understood in the direct democracies of classical Greece, retains a central position as the most substantial source for the concepts and arguments whereby people seek to explain, justify, guide or amend the public life of the community. Political thought remains the fundamental source of the material of political disputation.

8

Talking and writing, peoples and elites

Verbal debate and discussion is by comparison in modern states, a relatively private activity, though at the same time it remains the immediate language of power; it is speech that is the means of communication within the elite. Writing is in at both the beginning and the end of the game, and its relation to speech is symbiotic. The speech of the elite is derived from writing, and in the end its power is the power to influence what is subsequently written. It is written argument that has the longer term, wider effect, even though it may sometimes do so through the medium of speech, and through first influencing the speech of the elite.

It has been suggested that the 'novel, the movie, and the TV program' may have 'gradually but steadily, replaced the sermon and the treatise as the principal vehicles of moral change'.[6] There are two different forms of communication here. The first is less new than is claimed, and the theatre should be added to it, as an ancient and enduring place for the elaboration of political argument. The television programme is another matter. It briefly reports views which have been more substantially developed elsewhere. There may be ten people who hear about a book for every one who reads it, and a hundred who learn of it through a brief published reference, a review, or a reference on radio or television. Yet of these popular means of communication, the written word is both the most lasting and the most influential in the formation of ideas in the first place.

Were political activity confined entirely within a small elite, it is conceivable that written political argument would be of little significance. The conversation, the lunch, the memo, the letter, the telephone and the E-mail network would provide all the communication and persuasion necessary. There is a political thought of the public space, and a political thought of government. The second is composed of constitutional and legal reasoning, which will from time to time become public, but is not directed in the first instance to a public audience, but rather to the far smaller world of governing society. But the presence of an electorate whose votes must be won or retained, of citizens whose support must be cultivated, and of subjects whose contribution to the continuation of the political system must be ensured, means that politics never can be so confined either in its subject matter or in its method of expression.

The need for elites to go public in this way has consequences for the agenda of political thought. The more regularly democratic a polity becomes, the more likely it is that the mundane concerns of ordinary voters will become important parts of political argument. That means, in particular, the standard of living of the people, and its relation to accessible comparison. This does not mean that the cost of living will simply come to dominate political argument, or that argument will be based solely on the likely economic dividends of one manner of arranging things over another. Concern with the material standard of life is not an exclusive concern of democracy, or necessarily its dominant feature. But it is unlikely that such considerations can be ignored, and their place on the agenda is virtually guaranteed.

Political thought is an aspect of politics, and the more open and democratic that politics, the greater the contribution of political argument conducted in this way. At the same time a primary context for political thought is set by the broadening of politics so that with the extension of the vote between 1832 and 1928 it in some measure encompasses the entire adult population. That development was itself the occasion for extended debate: who was a citizen, what justification could there be for exclusion on grounds of sex, or religion, what was the character of the people and what consequences had the answer to that question for public stances on religion, culture, moral conduct and the laws governing them?

Political thought and political parties

Because of this association of political thought with arguments which presuppose some kind of goal to be pursued by debate or persuasion, political thought of the kind discussed in this book develops with a particular form of audience. Since the eighteenth century the importance of parliament and of an increasingly representative electorate as a forum for debate and criticism, and as the formal expression of a wider world of political contest, has meant that political thought has been directed towards an intelligent citizen, who is presumed to be either an elector or to have articulate aspirations to become one.

It is here that political parties have been of central importance. They have provided a meeting point for interests and ideas, potential vehicles for giving effect to both, and standards around which, in however loose an alliance, people of similar or related beliefs, aspirations and values might gather. The principles governing this clustering of ideas around parties have been historical as much as logical. It has not been the case either that one set of beliefs have dictated a set of electoral and governmental policies which follow logically from them, or that a group whose identity lies in its social situation has seen everything it seeks for epitomised in one clear exposition of political thought. The process has been more akin to that whereby a town grew up around a river crossing, or shops accumulate in a particular street. The existence of one shop attracts another, which attracts more. Hence the decline or disappearance of political parties can have consequences for political thought which owe nothing to the intellectual coherence of the ideas.

So conservatism with a small 'c', as a loose network of ideas, has been given a degree of stability by the existence of the Conservatism, with a capital 'C', of the Conservative Party. One of the features of the fragmentation and regrouping of liberal thought in the twentieth century was the erosion of a particular set of political alliances around which liberal political argument could loosely be centred. The decline of the Liberal Party after the First World War, and the slow emergence of Labour, were of more than simply electoral or ministerial significance. They gave shifting institutional focuses and forums for the conduct of political argument. That process of shifts and realignments has continued up to the present day, and some of the most important changes have occurred in the last quarter of the present century.

Even when politicians of an untypically reflective bent break from their parties, the general pattern is not disturbed. The major breach between Enoch Powell and the Conservative Party occurred over relations with the European Community. There was a further disagreement, at least of emphasis, over Northern Ireland, and a clear disagreement over nuclear weapons. But in each case, even when on one occasion Powell recommended voters to support the Labour Party, his arguments were clearly conservative ones, and even when he arrived at conclusions over policy which marked him off from his colleagues, he did so in a characteristically conservative manner.

The proposals for some form of proportional representation in parliamentary elections which were made with renewed energy at the beginning of the 1990s would therefore if implemented have consequences of far greater significance than the nonetheless important likely changes in the parliamentary basis of cabinet government, or the formation of government policy. In so far as they would give greater parliamentary representation and hence public voice and presence to parties whose electoral support had not been matched by their parliamentary seats, they would make possible shifts not just in the party system, but in the intellectual ambiences which form in loose association with political parties and within which parties operate. If proportional representation led to a change in the fortunes of the Liberal Democrat Party, there might well in the longer term be shifts in the intellectual composition, alliances and location of liberalism.

But political parties are still one thing, and political ideas another. There is both a connection and a distinction between conservatism as a loose alliance of political ideas, and Conservatism as the characterising features of those formally allied with the Conservative Party. It is necessary to avoid the danger into which the history of ideas may fall, of reducing ideas to the history of the organisations and movements with which they seem most frequently to be associated. Otherwise a history of conservatism becomes a history of the Conservative Party, one of socialism of a variety of sects, movements and organisations, whilst a history of liberalism slowly runs into the sands of the Liberal Party's twentieth century parliamentary decline.

In the nineteenth century, political thought was carried on across a world of freelance intellect and largely unprofessional opinion. By the first quarter of the twentieth, it was being carried on primarily within, or at least from within, the universities. The final creative phase for any political viewpoint is to move into the particular disciplines into which knowledge is divided, becoming an aspect of or viewpoint on the whole, rather than a discrete and external challenge. Thus feminism from the 1970s moved into the various disciplines of the academy, and a history of feminist argument becomes increasingly a history of feminist political theory, philosophy, jurisprudence, sociology, anthropology and historiography. Equally an examination of the New Right in the last quarter of the twentieth century must be principally concerned with writings which it would be reasonable to expect to find on university reading lists for economics or political science.

IV Statelessness

Matthew Arnold complained in 1869 that the British lacked a conception of the state as it was found on the continent, of 'the nation in its collective and corporate character, entrusted with stringent powers for the general advantage, and controlling individual wills in the name of an interest wider than that of individuals.'[7] For if there is one feature of British political thought which marks it off, if not from the political thought of North America, then from that of the rest of Europe, it is that it is stateless. The state does not exist in British political thought. It is easy to see why this should be so. The history of government in Britain, whilst characterised by more or less distinctive phases, has rarely been marked by sharp transitions of a kind which bring institutions sharply to the attention of those who are involved in or subordinate to them. There are four phases, but the history of each, and the succession of one by another, has been gradual and generally unobtrusive. First, government was both minimal and local. Second, it expanded by means of bureaucracy to govern more extensively both at home and in the empire. Third, whilst it extended at home, it played a part of decreasing importance on the international scene. And finally, as professionalism and management grew out of bureaucracy, the very shape and extent of both state and nation were qualified by involvement with the European Community. The period from the middle of the nineteenth century to the closing years of the twentieth encompasses not only the rise and fall of the empire and of class politics, but also the development of collectivism followed not so much by its demise, as by its reallocation from a centralised sovereign state to an increasingly dispersed number of agencies exercising legitimate power.

And that relocation of state powers within the wider European Community is happening at the oddest of times. The new awareness of being governed, and the fact of being governed within a political and economic community where awareness of the state and a conceptualisation of the state are commonplace, has introduced the idea into Britain for the first time with any widespread impact. Yet it has done so at a time when the British state in its traditional form is becoming of less importance. If political thought has ignored the state in Britain, will it ignore also its transformation or dilution at the end of the twentieth century? What will it have to say about the consequences for its traditional concerns of the permutations of sovereignty, and the changing patterns of legitimate government? It may be that stateless British theory is peculiarly appropriate for the Europe into which we are moving.

V Orthodoxy and Radicalism

Alone amongst the countries of Europe, Britain has lacked, since the seventeenth century, any revolutionary tradition. The essential distinction here is between radical methods and radical proposals. A political doctrine may be revolutionary in its tactics in the sense of insurrectionary, but thoroughly conservative in what it wishes to achieve. To be revolutionary in its proposals, it needs a confidence about the rightness of what it is seeking to establish as great as the confidence displayed by those whom it seeks to displace. The almost complete absence of any such revolutionary confidence explains why, for instance, proposals to abolish the monarchy have in Britain generally been half-hearted and apologetic. It may be true, as George Orwell wrote, that the life of the people is always lived against the dominant culture or even, as G. K. Chesterton suggested, that ordinary people listen carefully to the experts and then go and do completely the opposite. But if so that opposition has never gone beyond grumbles, criticisms and denunciations of existing customs, practices and arrangements. There have been no self-confident assertions of equally authoritative alternatives. On the one hand the radicals have been more reticent than in continental Europe. On the other, it has been easier for an orthodoxy or an establishment to present itself as the single national tradition, and all other views as ephemeral or alien. It was very much in this spirit that Margaret Thatcher when Prime Minister was able to speak of her intention of exorcising socialism from Britain and very much against it that A. J. P. Taylor presented a radical *tradition* in his book *The Troublemakers*.

This overwhelming weight of orthodoxy might seem to have been even stronger in the sphere of religion. An established church has been combined with religious organisation outside the Church of England which is, by comparison with the solid assurance of the national church, either peripheral or almost apologetic. But there have been both geographical and religious challenges to this quiet dominance. North of the English border, the combination of an established church with a region which despite its distinctive political and legal institutions is governmentally subject to London, has very different consequences for the authority of radical disagreement. This is why the 1990s were becoming so disconcerting for many in the British Isles. Assertive Islam, or self-confident religiously based social criticism in Scotland, were a challenge more akin to the Puritanism of the seventeenth century than to the polite nonconformity of the twentieth.

VI Ideology and Idealism

Political thought is better seen as a feature of politics than as simply either a reflection on politics or a moral or analytical premise from which political action springs. It is more appropriately understood as a principal characteristic of politics, rather than as something abstracted from politics. Viewed as a dimension of politics it can have something of both reflection and first principle but is not a separate sphere in the way that a theory of simple one way causality suggests.

If an idealist theory of the primacy of ideas does not provide an adequate understanding of the relation between political thought and political practice, neither does a theory of political thought as ideology. The ideological explanation, that ideas are an expression of material interests or social circumstances, particularly when combined with a structural theory of society, would lead one to expect far less variety and debate than has actually occurred.[8] Indeed so much diversity has there been, that if ideas were to be explained solely as arising from social structures, then neither Marxism nor class theory, but only a deeply variegated pluralism would provide an adequate account.

In order to grasp the place of political thought in politics, it is necessary to see it both as a distinct activity and as one which is never carried out in isolation. There are no hermetically sealed compartments, and just as an idea can appear attractive because it justifies something that a party or group already has other reasons for wishing to do, so at the same time it can present possibilities which had not previously been appreciated, or impose new moral or practical limitations. There has never been a merely one way traffic in any direction. So neither the idealist nor the materialist approach has an adequate grasp of politics, quite apart from their other limitations. They fail to see that politics, as an activity distinctive but never separate, is not reducible to the reflex of either ideas or interests. Political thought, therefore, is something which is frequently conducted by entrepreneurs who are simultaneously engaged in the activity of persuading, are concerned over public issues, and want to arrive at understanding or accounts of politics in general terms. To see Bernard Bosanquet, or F. A. Hayek, or Harold Laski, as solely either study bound intellectuals, or political persuaders, or partisan advocates is to miss the point that their work contained dimensions of all three.

One of the most useful ways of understanding the place of political thought in politics is through a modified use of Weber's theory of elective affinity. Groups choose or elect bodies of thought because of their appropriateness to the objectives they are already in part pursuing. But the interests of the group do not explain the ideas, nor do the ideas call into being the groups. Political thought is an activity which is carried on as part of politics, but which has its own dynamisms. Its developments and inventions can widen the contexts of opinion, and increase the range of available perspectives.

Political ideas can be published yet remain largely dormant for many years, and when they suddenly take life, it will frequently be in association with some group, class, interest or institution to whose purposes they seem appropriate. Yet at the same time they can inform or redefine those purposes, give people reasons and goals they did not previously have or were not previously aware of. So ideas can work indirectly, and permeate politics like water in limestone. It is necessary to remember, finally, that a major context for all the arguments about politics discussed in this book, consists of all the other arguments. Conservatism is developed, in part, in response to socialism, or socialism in response to liberalism.

VII Organising Themes

The themes which I describe and discuss in the following chapters are historical phenomena rather than logical ones. That is to say, the various segments and varieties of socialism, or conservatism, or liberalism or feminism in Britain over the last hundred and fifty years, exist and relate to each other in the way that they do, not because they express some logically prior principle from which they all necessarily flow, but because of a series of historical conjunctures. Logic and reason were not absent, but they did not determine the resulting pattern or character of the argument. Beliefs, aspirations and aversions, which for instance characterise conservatism at one time, will not characterise it at another, nor will it share identical goals with conservatives in other

17

places, but may indeed have characteristics which, if they are ever to be found at other times or in other places, are not to be found amongst conservatives at all.

W. H. Greenleaf has used the metaphor of character to express this diversity within unity: different aspects of conservatism, socialism, etc. are related to each other in the same way as the different traits of an individual's personality.[9] It is in many ways a fruitful analogy, although it suggests rather too much coherence, even of a non-logical kind. Were any individual racked by the kinds of disagreements and antipathies that have been found even within a single historical body of thought such as conservatism, let alone within the politics of the country as a whole, her sanity would not have lasted a day.

All attempts to categorise or classify political ideas have to confront the impossibility of fitting everything in. However the divisions are made, there are people and arguments which seem out of place. Equally affinities keep emerging between positions which had seemed at first to be utterly opposed to one another. Political ideas can, for instance, be divided into two broad types: those based on individuality, where politics and government are never more than an agency for expressing and accommodating multifarious purposes; and those based on communities where there is a vision of what society is and ought to be, and where politics and government are a means of sustaining and achieving this. Agency and vision do not provide comprehensive alternatives, but they do provide poles within which ideas have been located. W. H. Greenleaf and Michael Oakeshott in their differing ways have employed this polarity, the one with his distinction between libertarianism and collectivism, the other with his division of regimes into associations of individuals each with their own purposes on the one hand, and enterprises with common goals or missions on the other.

But though such a scale takes one a little way, it can soon begin to break down in the face of unexpected differences and similarities between positions that at first glance looked either related or opposed. Both toryism and socialism employ the idea of community, which is a concept suggestive of collectivism or enterprise, though the first envisages a moral and cultural one, the second an economic one. And all the battles of political argument involved disagreement over the boundaries and composition of the community in which, by the processes of politics and government, everyone is involved. On the other hand, even the defenders of the individual do not see everyone as an individual. Even liberalism, unless it is to be world liberalism, has a conception of the national community. Equally the arguments of feminism, however radical, involve as much a dispute over the boundaries and composition of human communities, as over the forms of organisation which are to operate within them. But because women are the largest excluded group, the changes which would be brought about by an end to their oppression are likely to be the most radical of all, overturning in application of detail, even if not in principle, all the institutions of existing political ideologies.

The remainder of this book consists of six chapters, together with a brief conclusion. Chapters 2 to 5 discuss conservatism, liberalism, socialism and feminism, whilst chapters 6 and 7 discuss the more recent developments of all of those bodies of argument in relation to property, markets and the economy, and to citizenship and political identity. Each chapter discusses its subject in general terms, looks at its principal historical phases, then discusses the principal issues with which political thought has been concerned. Although some of the issues will be the same for several chapters, some will be given attention in only one. For socialism, feminism, conservatism and liberalism differ from each other not only in the different things they say about the same topics, but in the topics to which some of them are alone in paying any serious attention at all. Even within the relatively short space of two centuries, and within the relatively limited geographical confines of the United Kingdom, not everyone is at all times and on all subjects conducting the same conversation, or pursuing the same argument.

2

CONSERVATISM

I General Remarks: Particular Character, Problems, Pre- and Misconceptions

Modern conservatism has always had two very different ways of presenting itself, one as King Henry, the other as Prince Hal. The first is as the normal, central, mainstream tradition of political thought. Such a presentation is of conservatism as the rightly dominant manner of thinking about government and politics, defending ground which is both middle and high against deviant, marginal and foreign heresies. The second style is very different, and takes the guise of a bold and rebellious voice crying in a wilderness laid bare by orthodoxies either socialist or liberal. A mixture of Puck and Jeremiah, it sees itself as in deepest opposition to the spirit of the times, and either playing knock down ginger on the front doors of the intellectual and cultural establishment, or standing in the market place and boisterously but without much hope calling the nation to repentance. Conservatism has thus been more flexible than its rivals, and has enjoyed the great tactical advantage of being able to adopt whichever of the two forms, confident and established, or radical and outraged, seemed most advantageous. Both liberalism and socialism, however they have been presented by their critics and opponents, have normally seen themselves only in the second role, as radical voices calling for change rather than as defensive ones asserting the values of existing beliefs or practices.

Liberalism, being ever a matter of principled aspiration, could rarely find sufficient indigenous laurels on which to rest, whilst it was only in the twentieth century that reference to the authority of established and working socialism became possible. But since this possibility depended upon both the example and the ethos of 'actually existing socialism' first in the Soviet Union and, after the end of the Second World War, in eastern Europe, it was not one which most socialists in Britain found either attractive or appropriate. Conservatism, too, had its unappealing foreign manifestations, but since it had other, domestic, grounds on which to base an argument which appealed to fact rather than to possibility, such uncongenial excesses could be easily marginalised and dismissed from the discussion. And the more that conservative arguments were grounded on traditions which were both national and particular, the more the examples of what was done in other countries could be set aside as simply irrelevant.

Despite its flexibility however, the predominant mode of modern British conservatism has been quiet and defensive. Even when it has been loud and assertive, it has still more frequently rallied to the defence of old interests than to the promulgation of new doctrines. In this it has differed from the combative conservatisms of continental Europe or North America. Its defensive character has been an aspect of its security. It was entirely in character, if breathtakingly proprietorial, when the conservative apologist F. J. C. Hearnshaw remarked in 1933, 'I suppose the best textbook of British conservatism is the constitutional history of England'.[1] For all its occasional presentation of itself as the eccentric defender of unfashionable truths, British conservatism has always celebrated values and institutions which have been powerfully entrenched, and which have never faced any serious radical challenges. In this too it has differed from conservatism in countries such as France or Spain. Even at its most shrill, defensive conservatism has never suffered from its critics any more than a slight to the pre-eminence of its values. It has never had to contest on equal terms with beliefs which calmly and confidently viewed its claims as partisan or absurd. This is not only because conservatism has successfully presented itself as the starting point for any argument, but because its opponents have generally portrayed themselves as the exponents of unfashionable doctrines whose foundations lay either in general principle or in foreign example, rather than as the custodians of alternative, equally entrenched, British traditions.

In one version of history, conservatism is either the political thought of the unthinking, a simple matter of dull custom or, when it is more conscious and articulate, a matter simply of closing ranks in unfavourable circumstances. Ted Honderich has referred to a prominent conservative of the 1980s and 1990s, Roger Scruton, as 'the unthinking man's thinking man'.[2] Andrew Gamble has shrunk conservatism to fit under the dismissive heading, 'Reaction'.[3] Albert Hirschman, most recently, has depicted conservatism in terms of three rhetorical and exaggerated responses to change: perversity, futility and jeopardy.[4] This is a myth nurtured by both the friends and the enemies of conservatism, though serving different purposes for each. F. J. C. Hearnshaw commented that conservatives 'do not always appear to be so wise as they are',[5] and Michael Oakeshott admiringly contrasted the 'conservative disposition' with the taste of others for abstract thought and rationalist theorising.[6] But conservatism has never been the stupid party's doctrine. Nor has it been a phenomenon composed entirely of instinct, disposition, custom, or inarticulate convention. Had it been so, it might be subject matter for psychologists or historians of culture and mores, but it would be of no interest to students of political thought. But that has never of course been anything more than the street clothes of conservatism, worn to protect the inner intellect from the sleet and drizzle of the political outdoors. Conservatism has produced a literature as rich and as subtle as that of its opponents. But it has often tried to pretend that it was not doing so, as in Hearnshaw's almost boastful and certainly inaccurate remark that 'the comparative inarticulateness of conservatives also explains the comparative scantiness of conservative literature'.[7]

Conservatism as a theory of order

Conservatism has been a theory of social and political order. It is this which has united Henry and Hal conservatism. For the one, order is historical and provides the structure and character of the life of the nation. For the other order is natural, a reality which will always break through the pretensions of dreamers and theorists. Conservatives have often distinguished their own beliefs as committed to order in preference to other values such as progress, or equality, or liberty. But it is more accurate to say that conservatism is a conception of order achieved by a particular means.

Social order may be sought in a number of ways. Whereas for an anarchist order is achieved by co-operation and fraternity, and for certain kinds of liberal by the rational pursuit by individuals in society of their own interests, for conservatives it is achieved, or more likely preserved, by tradition, hierarchy, deference, and the recognition and application of excellence and its concomitant inequality. This conception of order informs conservative thinking on society, on economics, and on politics. In all these spheres, order is to be achieved by the deference of the ordinary person to the extraordinary. Those who were distinguished by their finer understanding of the central values which gave society its distinctive quality, should have both the duty and the right to instruct and inspire their less enlightened fellows. For Edmund Burke at the end of the eighteenth century this superiority had taken the form of monarchy and aristocracy. It was this order, based on the preponderance of aristocracy in a mixed and inherited constitution with a deferential populace, which he defended against radicalism and revolutionary principles at the time of the French Revolution. There was, he wrote in 1791, a natural aristocracy in any society. The majority of a country's inhabitants would be 'in that state of habitual social discipline, in which the wiser, the more expert, and the more opulent conduct, and by conducting enlighten and protect the weaker, the less knowing, and the less provided with the goods of fortune.'[8] For Samuel Taylor Coleridge in the early years of the following century, superior wisdom and responsibility were to be found in a 'clerisy', 'the learned of all denominations'. For Thomas Carlyle excellence was to be found in aristocracy and priesthood, though not any aristocracy or any priesthood. Recent European history was, for Carlyle, proof that 'False Aristocracies are insupportable; that No-Aristocracies, Liberty-and-Equalities are impossible; that true Aristocracies are at once indispensable and not easily attained.'[9] The assumption underlying all these arguments was that there were wisdoms and truths to be sought, and that they held good for all of a society's members. There was no room in such a view for cultural or religious pluralism, and disagreement, particularly if it came from outside the charmed circle, could easily be explained away as the result of ignorance, inexperience or stupidity. In a classic statement of this view, the journalist Walter Bagehot advised his reader, whom he assumes to be 'an accomplished man' to put 'what seems to him most obvious, most certain, most palpable in intellectual matters' to his servants. They will be found to disagree, greater proof than which was not needed of the incapacity of the common people for public responsibility.[10]

In the twentieth century this conception of a social order whose development was historical rather than rational, and which was to be understood by living in it rather than by applying scientific principles to it, was exemplified in Michael Oakeshott's account of what he termed 'the pursuit of intimations'. Social life was not to be summed up in rules or blueprints, but there were nonetheless conventions which had arisen, and which could be slowly understood, rather in the manner that the common law was slowly understood, by the accumulation of experience of its detailed practices.

II Historical Setting

The truth of the conventional picture of conservatism as no more than a response to the natural or historical order of things is limited to a feature which, in one way or another, characterises most if not all political argument. Conservatism in Britain has

24

developed in response to events external to itself. It has been a reaction to some of the great transformations and threatened transformations of the last two hundred years. The first response, to revolution and democracy, was followed by a second, to liberalism and industrial capitalism, a third, to socialism, a fourth to bolshevism and revolution after 1917 and to soviet communism after 1945, and a fifth to parliamentary social democracy. Each made the character of conservatism more complex, and introduced further strands, far from consistently, into the overall weave. This process of accumulation and adaptation has meant that doctrines and aspirations which at one time had seemed anathema to conservatives, at a later date were treated with sympathy or even commendation when the principal threat or the most active antagonist was detected in a new quarter.

In so far as conservatism is a reaction to threatening change, rather than a more positive or independent exposition of values, it might seem strange to begin a discussion of recent political thought with it. But if the occasion for the elaboration of conservative values is reactive rather than active, those values are nonetheless closer to the character of dominant groups and institutions, more characteristic not so much of society or culture, as of those persons and institutions in commanding positions within them, than are the values of any of conservatism's opponents or rivals. The study of conservatism is to that extent the natural place to begin a study of political thought in general.

Conservatism has been a doctrine of power. That is not to say that those who have developed conservative arguments have necessarily done so whilst enjoying political power, or that their thinking is to be dismissed as merely in service to dominant persons, institutions or interests. But conservative thinking has generally proceeded from the assumption either that power is concentrated in the hands of those most worthy of wielding it, or that there is a readily identifiable group or category to whom it ought to be granted. Conservatism has been concerned to tease out the principles underlying existing institutions, and to justify them, rather than to speculate about alternative ways of doing things. Its history is thus not so much related more closely to the history of Britain than that of other doctrines, as related in a particular way, and in a manner which illuminates success rather more than it does aspiration, insiders rather more than outsiders, and rulers rather more than either rebels or ordinary citizens.

The first reaction of conservative thought was to the French Revolution. Conservatives, and they were not alone in this, saw the events in France as having major implications for politics and political thought in the British Isles. Insularity was challenged at the same time that tradition was threatened. The rise of popular politics and the overthrow of ancient institutions which it threatened, were met both by a condemnation of events in France, and by a defence at home of monarchy and aristocracy, as well as of established religion, habitual deference and social and political hierarchies. Social unity and continuity over time were asserted against the demand for rational appraisal or audit of institutions and, where they failed this scrutiny, their mechanical reconstruction or replacement. The disagreements were principally social, cultural and political, rather than economic. Yet though conservatism in Britain was a reaction to an event which had international repercussions, and was itself part of those international repercussions, it has always been more idiosyncratic and nationally particular than either socialism or liberalism, and has always placed itself less consciously within the international context of ideas. That is not to say that it has not drawn on ideas from abroad, but its presentation of itself has always been as something rooted in a particular culture, and drawing from that culture's history, rather than from frontier-hopping intellect. The reasons for rejecting the revolution in France were to be found in France, just as those for resisting radicalism and democracy at home were domestic.

The second reaction of conservative thought was to industrialism and liberalism, which were seen as morally atomistic and hence corrosive of social order and public responsibility. The liberal threat was a two-headed application of the notion of individual liberty. One head threatened political order by proposals for extensions of the franchise, the other threatened social order by detaching the idea of property from the notion of public duty, facilitating what for conservatives was a selfish and irresponsible use of wealth. 'Popular government', as it was termed by Sir Henry Maine, could never be anything other than the rule of the worst, the government of those who had neither the public virtue nor the skill and intelligence to act wisely. Property, it was argued, was a trust, not a personal possession devoid of public duties or responsibilities. W. H. Mallock, in his 1878 *The New Republic*, argued for a socially responsible use of wealth, a manner of conduct which could be expected from an aristocracy, but which was demonstrably lacking from the new liberal manufacturing and commercial classes. Disraeli praised the aristocracy of England 'which absorbs all aristocracies, and receives every man in every order and every class who defers to the principle of our society, which is to aspire and excel'.[11] With the reply to liberalism and industrialism, conservatism thus developed an economic dimension which had been absent from its earlier statements. The economic stance, however, was one which denied economic life any autonomy from the wider life of society, and which subordinated economic conduct to the moral duties which its possession imposed.

The third conservative response, to socialism, which developed in the last quarter of the nineteenth century, lacked a specifically political dimension, and was predominantly economic and social. Whereas against liberalism conservatives had argued for political power and property as trusts, against socialism they argued for the public benefits which arose from the unaccountable private pursuit of wealth, the very blemish which they had attributed to liberalism. But these benefits were no mere secondary consequences of the accidents and good fortunes of the market. They were a consequence of allowing full rein to the ambition of superior brains in the production of the nation's wealth. Inequality as both an inescapable and a beneficial characteristic of human life, especially human productive life, was asserted against socialism's promulgation of the second part of the great revolutionary triad of liberty, equality and fraternity. Once again, it was Mallock who made the case most eloquently, arguing for the necessity of what he termed 'directive ability' to energise the otherwise inert components of land, labour and capital, and for inequality to arouse the ambitions of the capable. And just as socialism, despite its strikingly British character, was seen by many of its opponents as an international rather than a domestic doctrine, so the conservative response to it began to draw on wider, European sources. Not only was Marx read in order to identify the theoretical roots of the threat to capital, but his elitist critics, Pareto and Michels, were read in order to find arguments for its defence.

The challenge of revolution had come from abroad, and of liberalism and socialism, although domestically based, from a point often at some distance from the centre of governmental power. By 1924 conservatives faced a Labour government, minority and brief though its tenure of office was, which formally espoused socialism and which thus brought what had previously been a challenge from the wings onto the centre of the political stage. What could be contained between the two world wars, finally gained legitimate control of the machinery of state in 1945 with a majority Labour government which proceeded to implement a social democratic programme. As with 1789, 1945 provided a seismic shudder to the conservative intellect which released an avalanche of restatements and developments of the case in favour of responsible property ownership, and against ambitious government. Quintin Hogg argued that private property was 'the natural bulwark of liberty because it ensures that economic power is not entirely in the hands of the State', Michael Oakeshott that 'The government of a collectivist society can tolerate only a very limited opposition to its plans'.[12]

The response of conservatism to social democracy was paralleled by that to very different political movements in eastern Europe. The Russian Revolution of October 1917 had established an order whose ideology appeared to threaten regimes throughout the capitalist world, and which sponsored within other countries political movements working for the revolutionary overthrow of capitalism. When this was combined with the more conventional aspirations of a powerful European state, a double-sided enemy emerged which exemplified both foreign imperialism and minatory doctrine. The Russian seizure of power across a broad swathe of territory in eastern Europe at the end of the Second World War in 1945 inaugurated an intensification of this threat. The response within conservatism was able to unite patriotism on the international level with the defence of property and markets and of a deferential culture at home. The Soviet Union, before the reforms which ended Russian hegemony after 1989, provided conservatism with a perfect foil in its attack upon social democracy. The parliamentary proposals of democratic socialists could be presented as simply the Sunday-best clothing of a personage whose true attire was to be discovered in the mundane work-clothes of eastern European despotism.

The collapse of eastern European state socialism after 1989 was an event as significant for conservatism as the original Russian Revolution of 1917, or the French Revolution of two centuries before. It changed the reference points for political navigation, and posed conservatism the same kind of problem, at least at the level of debate, as would be posed to a revivalist preacher by the abolition of hell. An entire demonology was swept aside, whilst the very term 'conservative' became applied to views in eastern and south-eastern Europe and the former Soviet Union as diverse as hard line party communism on the one hand and savagely racist nationalism on the other.

If conservatism had been, whenever it was articulated, a response to threats or challenges, the last two decades of the twentieth century presaged the greatest challenge of all: the removal of any enemy against whom to mount a defence of conservative values, and the disappearance of any stimulus to their exposition or development.

III Society

Conservatism, though a political stance, is as much rooted in a conception of society as in one of government. So Quintin Hogg was able in 1947 to distinguish conservatives, for whom politics was an instrumental and secondary matter, from all those others who made it an activity worth pursuing in its own right. Amongst conservatives, said Hogg, 'the simplest among them prefer foxhunting – the wisest religion'.[13] For conservatives, there is a world of social life conducted through institutions and corporations of one kind and another with which politics has little or nothing to do. But at the same time, the state should defend these institutions, and should be partial on their behalf: the conventional patriarchal family household, the established church, even fox-hunts. But not communes, or non-Christian faiths, and certainly not trade unions.[14]

So government, whilst on the one hand intervening as little as possible in educational institutions such as schools or universities, was on the other obliged to make sure that they acted to transmit the central traditions of a culture whose character and limits did not allow for either substantial variety or substantial dissent. Whilst liberals or socialists viewed education as liberating or empowering individuals, for conservatives education had the dual role of training in useful skills, and transmitting an established culture.

Nation and family

The society which conservatives had defended against both revolution and liberalism had been a public one of noble and responsible leaders, and deferential albeit aspirant masses. The defence against revolution and democracy after 1789 had involved the consolidation of social order, deference and religion, whilst the defence against liberalism had involved the consolidation of paternalism and aristocracy. But as a slow accommodation with democracy made the advocacy of hierarchies of social power, respect and worthiness increasingly difficult, conservatism stressed first the nation and then the family as the expressions of a deference and a paternalism which it was now difficult to defend in the form of superior persons. Particularly in the defence against socialism, the family came to perform an increasingly important role as both banner and shield of conservatism.

Nation as culture

Liberalism and egalitarianism, it was argued, both dissolved and misunderstood the interlocking hierarchies of knowledge and control which characterised society. And since for conservatives the nation, which was the highest level of social association, was defined by tradition and by established institutions and values, there was always incipient within conservatism a sense of national identity and hence of the alien, the deviant and the subversive. Nationalism had emerged in nineteenth century Europe as revolutionary and radical, but by the end of the century a conservative and imperial version of the doctrine was available both to justify the international claims of states, and to reassure them when threatened by the similar ambitions of others. Liberal internationalism with its conceptions of universal rationality threatened the conception of national distinctiveness, whilst socialism, in so far as it was internationalist or revolutionary, was actively hostile to the idea of nationalism, suspecting it as a legitimising mythology for capitalism and reaction.

Nation and family were given increasing emphasis in the twentieth century as the social hierarchies of rank and respect became difficult to defend. In matters of culture, morality and family life, the growth within Britain of a cultural diversity in the second half of the twentieth century which was openly plural rather than stratified or hierarchic was accompanied by an insistence that some ways of life were to be preferred to others. The family and the culture for which it served as both image and incubator, became for conservatives the tangible expression of the nation as Empire departed, as immigrants arrived, and as Celtic nationalism threatened the bland elision of England and Britain.

Family and sexuality

So conservatism came upon the family relatively late. Aristocracy as a principle as much of statecraft, public leadership and property owning as of social and domestic life, had a far more sure footing in conservative hagiography. Families, in the sense of idealised households, were altogether more middle class and mundane, and did not acquire promotion into the sanctum of values until the accommodation to democracy was well established.

The family has been regarded by conservatives as both natural and beneficial, and representing in microcosm many of the aspects of the broader conservative understanding: authority, subordination, paternalism, divisions of power and function. In so far as a defence of the family was a defence of gender divisions, conservatism was at its least distinctive. Its concern in the nineteenth century was with the authority of fathers. By the end of the twentieth century, this had been replaced by the responsibilities of mothers as the principal conservative line on the family. But the division of powers and functions remained the same.

Against a liberal social and moral theory which saw 'private' or domestic lives as matters of individual choice, conservatives argued that they were an historical creation, and the idea that they could be chosen at will or at random in some kind of moral or domestic bazaar was to misunderstand the nature of human social life itself. And though such historical growth might create variety, it did so only around a central core in respect of which other forms were peripheral. The responsibility of government was therefore not to act as an impartial enforcer of voluntary contracts, but rather to be a third party to domestic arrangements, or a political over-parent to families, encouraging and upholding by the use of law and other powers of the state the powers of parents over children and husbands over wives, and, conversely, discouraging or prohibiting forms of association which departed from the conservative norm.

The idea of individuality or personality as matters of both personal responsibility and historical creation avoided two opposing theoretical traps. On the one hand was universalism or, as conservatives like Michael Oakeshott called it, rationalism, on the other, relativism. A universal standard of personal conduct, it could be objected, ignored the particular character and development of real societies, which could be intensely varied. On the other hand if existing customs or practices were to be the only moral criterion, then there was no basis for a moral appraisal of anything, since whatever was done was good. The way between these two positions was to argue that whilst good practices were traditional, not all practices were equally good or truly rooted in tradition. This was illustrated by the account given in the last quarter of the twentieth century of sexuality. Roger Scruton was able in 1986 to present an argument in favour of 'normal' sexual conduct which avoided either relativism or rationalism.[15] Relativism was avoided because some traditions and practices were preferred to others, rationalism because individual choices could only be understood in the context of the particular historical traditions within which they were made and which alone could give them meaning.

Such arguments were stated with particular force in the 1970s when changes in the law on abortion and homosexuality had given women greater control over their own reproduction, and adult men more control, or the state less, over their sexual conduct in private. In each case the ideal of sex as both marital and principally for the production of children was challenged. It was thus a Conservative government which in 1988 accepted a clause in its Local Government Bill prohibiting the 'intended promotion' of homosexuality as a 'pretended family relationship'. What was threatened by all these changes, amongst other ideals, was that of the patriarchal family.

Religion

Conservatism has been associated with the established Protestant church. But within Protestantism there have been two competing conceptions of authority. On the one hand has been the episcopal theory of the special powers and responsibilities of the priesthood, organised in a hierarchy led by bishops, on the other various conceptions of the 'priesthood of all believers', of the democratic authority of the whole congregation of the faithful, or at least of the oligarchic authority of lay elders, the presbyters of Presbyterianism. Conservatism has been a defender of episcopal rather than Presbyterian authority. Evangelical Protestantism and the concept of the priesthood of all believers were not readily compatible with social and political doctrines which stressed inequality, and the restriction of insight and skill to a minority.

Christian, English speaking, paternalistic family life was not simply one version amongst many, but the valued norm which ought positively to be acknowledged and supported, and from which all other forms should be regarded as deviant. Such assertions were not of course new. Henry Fielding's Mr Thwackum had expressed the view that 'When I mention Religion, I mean the Christian Religion; and not only the Christian Religion, but the Protestant Religion; and not only the Protestant Religion, but the Church of *England*.'[16] But in the eighteenth century, the assertion was against faiths, and lack of faith, which could be more readily dismissed as either the curiosity of foreigners or the failings of natives.

Conservatism was like other forms of political argument in its gradual secularisation. At the beginning of the nineteenth century religion provided both a language and a set of values for the conduct of public argument. By the end of the first quarter of the twentieth century, whilst conservatives still spoke of the importance of religious practice, it was as an aspect of good conduct, rather than as either its foundation or context.

Religion for conservatives involved a recognition of the limited character of all secular achievement and, properly understood, restrained ambitions for worldly perfection. But religion has never occupied the same place in English as in continental conservatism. The broad protestantism of the Anglican Church has provided a non-secular reference point for conservatives. But because there have always been other denominations within the Christian community, Anglicanism could never become as solidly a part of conservatism as could more secular values. And because nonetheless Britain was not divided along lines either of religion or sectarianism, the assertiveness of continental conservative uses of religion did not develop here. From the early quiet confidence of the assured place of the Church of England, there developed as one element within conservative beliefs about religion a different view, of religion as a private affair which, though it should be respected by politicians and governors, had no consequences for the way in which they conducted their public actions. Enoch Powell argued that there was no 'gospel of general benevolence or charity' to be derived from Christianity.[17]

But by the last quarter of the twentieth century, the presence of hitherto alien but confident faiths within the national community led to further revisions. The growth of Islam as an equally self-confident and assertive faith was part of a new pluralism which included the radical assertion of Protestant Christianity as part of a newly combative right wing argument. In the attacks on 'permissiveness' during the 1980s, the Conservative Family Campaign linked evangelical Protestantism, the patriarchal family, and conservative politics in an attack on liberals and socialists who had 'embraced the policies of social destruction'.[18]

IV Economy

Conservatives, when they have advocated a hands-off policy by government towards the ownership and exchange of property, have done so not because they were indifferent to the consequences or believed in individual rights to use property for the untrammelled pursuit of self-interest, but because they believed they knew what the consequences would be of a state which defended existing distributions of economic power. For not only ought property to be a trust, but when allowed to flow naturally it would accumulate according to the moral and talent contours of society. Its distribution would not in general be random, whatever individual idiosyncrasies there might be, and wealth would tend to be attached to worth and to facilitate its cultivation.

This was an historical and traditional justification of property, rather than a utilitarian one. The idea that human life or social arrangements could be directed or arranged at will or according to either abstract principles or individual whim had generally been seen as anathema to conservatives from Burke to Oakeshott. That which we own, we hold in trust between our predecessors and our successors. A justification therefore of

money and markets as rational, mechanical devices for registering choices or rewarding enterprise is not one which sits easily in
an otherwise conservative set of aversions and aspirations.

Yet it was over the economy and over property that conservatism was most divided, defending property as a trust in its
response to liberalism, whilst in its response to socialism adopting an almost utilitarian resistance to the threat of controls and
redistribution. Property as a trust was most frequently presented as held by some form of aristocracy; property as a reward for merit and an encouragement to its pursuit and
cultivation was more usually envisaged as vested in families.
But whether in their aristocratic or their bourgeois mode conservatives, in so far as they have appealed to the beneficial
consequences of wealth rather than of the wealthy, have always
done so in the context of their distinctive conception of an
inegalitarian social order.

It was argued by William Cobbett that labour was a form of
property. This had worrying implications for conservatives,
since it created a form of property distribution which was inherently inalienable, and an egalitarian distribution which
whilst it might be marginally modified, could only be substantially affected by death. The difficulty was faced and dealt with
by W. H. Mallock, who redefined labour as an inert resource
which, like land and capital, could only be given active force or
value by the far more thinly distributed quality of directive
ability. Rephrasing Locke, he envisaged an economy where
labour, instead of being mixed with the material world to create
property, itself became malleable material in the hands of an
elite. Such an elite of responsible men of property was celebrated
in conservative thinking from Mallock through Baldwin to the
tories of the late twentieth century.

Conservative economic thinking has meant that on the one
hand whilst there may be an aversion to public ownership, there
is not a doctrinaire objection to it. The arguments against
twentieth century nationalisations were, for conservatives, derived more from a view of the state than from a view of the
economy. On the other hand, when conservatives defended markets, they did so as much in support of the social and political

autonomy of groups and associations and institutions, as in application of any economic theory. When conservatives have been involved in more economic, liberal defences of the market, it has been as a result of a political, tactical alliance rather than of an intellectual one.

There were members of the Conservative Party, such as Enoch Powell in the 1960s and 1970s or Keith Joseph in the 1980s, who praised and advocated economic markets. But though their arguments were often accompanied by familiar conservative ones about national traditions setting the context within which economic activity took place, or about the duty of government to make provisions for need outside the sphere of markets, the character of their economic proposals, when taken by themselves, belonged to the liberal tradition, even though party labels suggested otherwise.

V State, Government and Authority

Government can be distinguished from politics, even though one is hardly conceivable without the other. Government is the exercise of legitimate power, the issuing of commands, the enforcement of laws and policies. Politics consists of all those activities – argument, lobbying, organising campaigns, voting, plotting – which seek to influence, amend, obstruct or control the activity of government. In terms of such a distinction conservatism is, together with feminism, the least political of the major political stances, and the one which gives least relative weight to politics, just as socialism gives most. Government, on the other hand, is another matter entirely. Conservatism, it has often been pointed out, has been characterised by a secular equivalent to the Christian doctrine of the fall of man. Human beings were inherently flawed. This not only set limits to what could be achieved by the exercise of reason, but required the bulk of humanity to be ruled, in their own interests and those of everyone else, by a government which would check their more dangerous tendencies just as a firm parent sets limits to the follies and dangerous actions of children. After the French Revolution and in response to demands for extensions of the franchise in the nineteenth century, this belief enabled conservatives to argue that the aspiration towards equality rested on a misconception about the possibilities of human nature. People were not equal, and the most that could be hoped for was that the fortunate and more capable minority would be able to carry out a damage limitation exercise on the imperfections of the majority. In the twentieth century these views about the dangerous delusions of worldly perfection were the basis for an attack on what was termed 'ideology' or 'rationalism', and which meant in practice any use of general principles to argue for widespread social, economic or political reform.

As a doctrine of order and of inequality, conservatism begins with government rather than with politics. In responding to the French Revolution it was articulating a presumption in favour of authority with which, when in the nineteenth century it faced the challenge of democracy, it was able to set limits to the claims of popular government. So beginning with a resistance to republicanism and revolution, conservatism moved through a brake on democracy, to a resistance to the use of extended state power for economic management and social reform.

Conservatism before the French Revolution was concerned to expound an account of the constitution, of the sources of legitimate power, and of the grounds upon which obedience to that power could be demanded. The revolution in France represented for conservatives the overthrow of legitimate government, the alarming assertion of popular power, and the unwarranted extension of the power of the state. For much of the nineteenth century, and from time to time in the twentieth, the question of both the source of governmental authority and the proper location of governmental power continued to exercise conservatives. Whilst modern conservatism's germination may have been begun by revolution in France, its growth was nurtured by the uncertainties of growing democracy in Britain.

Conservatism has its modern origins in opposition to a democracy which was viewed as no more than the corrupt rule of the mob or of demagogues. Sir Henry Maine, in his discussion of *Popular Government*, wrote that democracy was no more than

'Monarchy inverted'.[19] But by the end of the nineteenth century, this hostility had been replaced by what is sometimes termed 'Tory democracy', an accommodation between noblesse oblige and an extended franchise. Benjamin Disraeli was able to describe that phase of the extension for which he was responsible, the Reform Bill of 1867, as a means of ensuring that 'the people are led by their natural leaders'.[20] W. H. Mallock made a similar case, employing the insights of the continental elitist theorists to argue that democracy could work, and could only work, by the masses recognising the superior powers of superior people. A twentieth century conservative pamphleteer could present the Conservative Party leader, and Prime Minister, Stanley Baldwin, as having a fatherly regard for ordinary people, and representing the old fashioned paternalism which recognised both their deficiencies and their needs and interests.[21]

A continuing strand in conservative thinking on the state is the view that government stands in a paternal relationship to its subjects. Government, in this view, is the institutional embodiment of the superior wisdom and heightened sense of public duty which was seen in aristocracy at its best. When the power of the House of Lords was challenged at the beginning of the twentieth century by a Liberal government intent on getting the 1910 'people's budget' through Parliament, it was from amongst Conservatives that the fiercest opposition to any diminution of the powers of the Upper House came. This was in part for the tactical reason that the Lords were a bastion of Conservative second line votes. But there was a wider argument too, that the Upper House represented impartial and responsible statesmanship, superior to the mere clash of party in the Commons. This responsibility is not normally so narrowly located. Government as a whole is taken to have a duty to ensure the well-being of all its subjects, and particularly of its poorest and most vulnerable. Hence for Enoch Powell the social services were an essential means of 'providing for the members of the community, or for a section of it, those conditions which community action, and only community action, can provide'. For Keith Joseph, even in his most lyrical defences of the market, there were things that 'government, and governments alone, can do'. By implication, at least, that included intervening to make sure that the strong did not 'beat up or eat up the weak'.[22]

This view is accompanied by a conception of the nation as unified on the basis of common traditions and institutions. It is a unified rather than plural association, and as such there are those who understand common culture and traditions, and those who do not. Whatever view conservatives have taken over public economic monopolies, the identity of the nation is firmly expropriated.

Such a view has two sides, one which involves obligations for rulers, the other obligations for citizens. But it is a view which is hostile to the idea of subjects as having rights, or of states as representative of those whom they rule. In some versions of twentieth century conservatism therefore, the obligation of the subject has been stressed to the point of almost complete eclipse of the responsibilities of rulers. If government is seen as the guardian of the best or highest interests of society, then the role of subjects is construed principally in the light of that activity. Their principal obligation, as Roger Scruton has put it, is to be ruled.

The attitude of conservatives towards intermediary associations between government and subject has therefore always been flexible. Institutions such as the family, or the church, or the school, if they are seen as inducting people in traditional values and forms of conduct, and giving them the opportunity for growing into their responsibilities, are seen as of great value. But if organisations or institutions are seen as sectarian, divisive, or subversive, they can be attacked with converse vigour. Even local government can be included in this condemnation if it can be seen as captured by minorities or sectarians, and in opposition to central government as the custodian of national values or purposes. Thus the conservative thinker Michael Oakeshott singled out trade unions in his 1949 essay on 'The Political Economy of Freedom' as 'labour monopolies' and as such 'more dangerous than any other'.[23]

The state does not derive its authority from those whom it governs, nor does its legitimacy arise from principles of either ethics or rationality. 'Regio, ergo sum.' It rests on two foundations. The first is tradition, which is sometimes a means of smuggling in that very rationalism and utilitarianism which conservatism responds to with such hostility when it appears in liberal thought. The institutions of government were not merely sanctified by time, but proved effective by their survival through it. Like the common law or Topsy, the constitution had 'just growed', and it existence was also its justification, giving it both the venerability of antiquity and the practical utility, denied to utilitarianism, of actually existing. They were not mechanical or rational creations, but a natural part of a society which was itself best seen as organic. The second foundation of government was the concentration of ability, understanding and, though this was less stressed in the twentieth century, virtue in a relatively few persons. In the nineteenth century this had meant aristocracy changing out of its landowning, country clothes into its city, governing ones. In the twentieth century it meant seeing government as the political expression of less socially precise forms of excellence, whether cultural or managerial. This notion, of the naturalness of government as a form of social guardianship or trust, sits alongside a belief that the proper functions of government are limited, and that politics and statecraft are at one and the same time the highest and the most marginal forms of human activity. On the one hand *la cuisine politique* exists only to provide good food. On the other, government is required because of the fallibility of human nature, especially of the human nature of ordinary humans. So for conservatives the essential personnel of government will always be composed of judges, police, soldiers and, for some, clergy. Such beliefs provide some grounds at least for justifying restrictions on local government as a capping of the powers of amateurs and demagogues, and resisting the powers of the European Community as a defence against those who have not been inducted in our own national traditions of rule.

VI Trailer

Whilst conservatism neither disappeared nor disintegrated in the final quarter of the century, it became involved in debates which placed severe strains on its character, as they did on the character of its opponents and rivals. For it became, in the alliance of arguments often referred to as the 'New Right', closely associated with an aggressive version of market liberalism. It was an association which was on occasion to prove both ideologically disconcerting and politically confusing.

But this apparent shift of emphasis within conservatism was far greater within Conservative Party politics than within conservatism as a body of political argument. The impression of new departures, in other words, is accentuated by a correspondence between the words which describe ideas and those which describe parties, by which conservatism alone is characterised by the end of the twentieth century.

Conservatism in the late twentieth century has been characterised as well by a far greater immunity to political ideas from outside the United Kingdom. Whilst market liberals, socialists and feminists have all drawn on an increasingly international body of writing, conservatives, as was appropriate to people who presented themselves as the untheoretical trustees of indigenous tradition, have made far less use, though even they have made some, of the frequently more militant versions of their beliefs which were current in North America and on the mainland of Europe.

3
LIBERALISM

I Introduction

Liberalism is a term which, like Roquefort, does not travel well. North American conservatives who attack what they call liberalism in the politics of their own country would be amazed to find the term being applied in Europe, and perhaps especially in the United Kingdom, to describe views very close to their own. This difficulty is a reminder that the meaning of such political titles is conventional and historical, rather than logical or absolute. Liberalism is what liberals believe. The problem for those who want to identify exactly what it is that liberals believe is made greater by the difficulty of identifying liberals. With socialists and conservatives, and even to some extent with feminists, there are parties, organisations or movements, the published views of whose members or supporters provide, if not a comprehensive picture, at least a starting point for enquiry.

The difficulty in the case of liberalism is that whilst in the nineteenth century there was a Liberal parliamentary politics, the twentieth century was marked by an increasing marginalisation of organised, party Liberalism. After 1918 the Liberal Party and its organisations became less and less substantial, less and less a visible starting point or rough marker. It was a malicious paradox of history that the doctrine which had been most committed to the political rights of citizens to control their own government, should benefit least, and suffer most, as democracy

43

was extended. Without the sheet anchor of a party connection, liberal ideas floated with far greater freedom, but also far greater partisan promiscuity. Increasingly from the end of the First World War, with the decline of the Liberal Party from its position as one of the two major parties in the land to that of a minor third player in a two party system, liberal ideas were increasingly free of any particular organisational or group attachments. Liberalism percolated into other traditions of political argument in a way the Fabians would have envied, and it has to be dissected out from its actual historical context before it can properly be seen. It permeated all manner of arguments, yet became a characterising feature of none. Socialism and conservatism have been able to liaise with government through parties which relate in differing degrees to socialist and conservative ideas. Liberalism has largely lost that connection, and liberal ideas have formed other liaisons: on the one hand, with other parties, and on the other with academic political theory in a way which has increased their theoretical sophistication without necessarily sharpening their polemical edge.

This has meant that liberalism has frequently appeared more dispersed than other bodies of political thought, despite their own lack of coherence. In the nineteenth century liberalism, despite its internal varieties of emphasis, was not divided between claims for apparently incompatible freedoms. Political rights, property, opportunity and a free constitution were each part of a loosely coherent network. By the middle of the twentieth century, at least four distinct strands of liberal political thought could be detected: an assertion of individual political, intellectual, moral and religious liberty; a defence of rights in the existing distribution of property or capital; a belief that the rights and powers that go with the possession of property are necessary and desirable for all individuals, and that if necessary the state should act in such a way as to make those rights and powers accessible to all; and a critical appraisal of constitutional arrangements, together with proposals for their improvement. The fragmentation of liberalism in the twentieth century has meant not only that these four elements are by no means regularly found together, but that they have often been found in conjunction with views and proposals which are not at all liberal.

The division in liberal thought is often presented as one between two different concepts of liberty: negative and positive. That is not always a helpful distinction. It may be possible to explain in terms of a negative/positive distinction, the difference between a defence of the existing distribution of property on the one hand, and the recommendation that property be distributed so as to promote the greatest possible equality in the enjoyment of its benefits on the other, or to see social reform as positive because it involves the use of public power to give individuals resources they had not previously possessed, whilst the use of state power simply to prevent any invasion of existing liberties is placed in the pigeon-hole of negative freedom. But the parcelling out of liberalism as advocating either negative or positive freedom cannot give an adequate understanding of a liberalism which for instance is involved with constitutional reform. Such 'constitutional liberalism' sees all social life as necessarily affected by the institutions of government, which are themselves artificial. The choice is not between doing nothing on the one hand, and seeking substantive effects on the other, but simply between doing things well in a way that benefits individual citizens by facilitating their self-government, and doing things badly or in a less than impartial way, so that either by design or incompetence, individual self-government is impeded.

All liberals believe that liberty is positive, in the sense that its exercise involves free action by individuals. They differ substantially in the extent to which they believe collective governmental action can increase, disseminate or facilitate liberty. What links them is an individualism which is both moral and methodological: moral in that normative or prescriptive argument proceeds from the basis of individual rights, methodological in that the descriptive analysis of human social life proceeds from an assumption that the principal actors and components are neither groups nor whole societies, but individual persons. Despite the diffusion of liberalism and the presence of liberal ideas in some very odd ideological company, those who identify themselves as liberal have in general distinguished themselves from socialists and conservatives whom they have stigmatised as sharing an undue fondness for government, or an insufficient respect for individual autonomy.

The individual persons from whom liberalism developed its arguments were both real, in that they were subjects and citizens of existing states, and ideal, in that the rights they were to enjoy were more often than not denied and aspired to, rather than actually possessed. So whilst Thomas Paine's invocation in 1791 of natural rights might be denounced by Jeremy Bentham as 'simple nonsense' Bentham, like Paine, employed the idea of the individual as someone with observable needs as the litmus paper for determining the utility or otherwise of existing systems of government. His 'felicific calculus' was presented as a rational method of determining the best policies and forms of government by calculating the balance of pleasure and pain that alternative courses of action would be likely to produce.

Liberal individualism has its problems. Liberalism is a doctrine of the public space, and of the proper function of the state within it. But it is also a doctrine of individuality, of the value of private, as opposed to public, activity. Yet though privacy is valued, its character is taken as given, and its uses and characteristics are not built into the doctrine. On the other hand, the naturalness of what occurs in the private sphere, without being asserted, is taken for granted. The structure and internal relations of the family, the relations between the sexes, the use of property, are all assumed to fall within this natural sphere, so that what exists, or would exist if the state fulfilled its proper obligations, is not itself subject to critical appraisal. This has meant that whilst on the one hand liberalism has taken the individual as the starting point, a number of unquestioned and frequently unstated assumptions about what constitutes an individual have been allowed to give shape to the argument. The ideal abstract individual has often been not only adult and property owning, but male, paternal and patriarchal. Liberals have often spoken of people when what they meant was male heads of households. This has left the female majority of the population inadequately accounted or catered for in liberal thought, absorbed or hidden as they have often been in liberal

46

thinking within the privacy of the household, of which the male head is treated as the only visible or public representative.

II Historical Setting

Despotism and liberty

Liberalism has, historically, been a continuous protest against restrictions on the self-determined actions of individuals. It began as an attack on state-created privilege, and an insistence on the rights of the individual against attempts by government to interfere in his or her religious, moral, cultural, economic or political choices or actions, provided always that those actions were performed within an agreed framework of rules which applied impartially to all and which, though they guaranteed procedures, were neutral as to substance or ends. Property might be the foundation of all other rights, but those rights were themselves a form of property. 'Every man is a proprietor in society,' wrote Paine, 'and draws on the capital as a matter of right.'[1]

Whereas conservatism's historical context was provided by revolutionary events abroad and radical proposals at home, liberalism developed as a criticism of the existing and established use of power within the United Kingdom. In so far as it identified others as usurpers or radicals, they were those who usurped or abused the powers of government, and who were radical in the extent to which they defended or extended their own privileges at the expense of their fellows. Its context has thus been principally a domestic or national rather than international one, and the circumstances against which it has reacted have been established and systematic restrictions, particularly those imposed by government, on the lives of individuals. But it was no more immune from the symbolic clash of alternatives overseas than was conservatism. There was a radical demand for reform in the North American colonies and a radical support for liberty in France in the eighteenth century, just as there was a conservative reaction against the overthrow of the French

47

monarchy after 1789. If conservatism was a response to the overthrow of the old regime, liberalism was a protest at its continuation. Edmund Burke was answered by Tom Paine, who in his *The Rights of Man* declared that there were 'two modes of government which prevail in the world', government 'by election and representation' and government by 'hereditary succession'. The first was known as a republic, and was based on 'Reason'; the second is monarchy or aristocracy, and was based on 'Ignorance'.[2]

Liberalism has had three principal phases. In the first, it protested against oppressive government. In the second it advocated an extended franchise. In the third it proposed methods for fitting an expanded electorate to its new responsibilities, not only materially but morally and culturally. In so doing it proposed ways in which a state, no longer seen as inherently hostile because controlled not by an aristocratic elite but by the people, could be employed for liberal ends.

At the mid point of the nineteenth century, the liberal approach to both politics and government seemed clear. In its ideal shape, the state was a necessary but conventional evil, constructed by free individuals to uphold a framework of law within which they might pursue their own ends to the betterment of themselves and, indirectly, of society as a whole. This was the intellectual legacy which the utilitarianism of Jeremy Bentham and James Mill passed on and which seemed to promise liberty to each and prosperity to all.

Such liberalism, despite its acceptance of the unfortunate necessity of government, emerged in opposition to much of what the state did in actual practice, both in its regulation of the economy and its maintenance of economic privilege, and in its discriminatory treatment of individual beliefs, particularly religious – or irreligious – ones. This was because the state that actually existed was constructed not on the basis of the rational defence of the interests of its subjects, but on aristocratic privilege, unjustified tradition and arbitrary custom. The corrective to the deficiencies of government as it existed, and the means of moving towards government as it should be, was a combination of rational reform and an extension of the franchise. When subjects had a vote which gave them control over their government, they would ensure that that government acted in a way which was consistent with their interests, rather than with the interests of some aristocratic faction.

Liberalism and democracy

But there were problems with this, and their solution was part of a liberal response to the extension of democracy which liberalism as a doctrine of political liberty implied. An earnest desire for moral and spiritual progress could not readily be satisfied with a notion of human life which seemed to offer no more than the piling up of material, sensual happiness. Moreover the liberty and prosperity which such liberalism promised, appeared from the growing researches of journalists and social scientists to be distributed with an unevenness that was equally offensive whether it was random or systematic. Both these difficulties applied with particular force if the extension of democracy brought large numbers of people within the political community. Intellectual and material poverty was of far greater significance if those who suffered it exercised political power. If liberals had attacked the tyranny of aristocracy, monarchy and privilege in part because it was exercised by the selfish and the incompetent, then the quality of the new electoral masters was of equal concern and needed cultivating with some care. Liberalism has always contained a recognition of the dangers of saying that freedom is no more than the unconstrained pursuit by people of whatever it is they happen to want. This view became prominent the moment that the expansion of the parliamentary franchise introduced into electoral politics people whose cultural experience and assumptions could not be guaranteed to match those of the previous, more limited, electorate.

To the problem of the quality of liberty, James Mill's son, John Stuart Mill, responded with a moral reformulation of utilitarian liberalism and an insistence on the moral and cultural dimension to the exercise of liberty. It was better to be a philosopher unhappy than a pig happy. There were standards, in other words, by which the use people made of their freedoms could be judged, and it was as much a matter of judgment to distinguish between higher and lower, as to distinguish between freedom and slavery. T. H. Green took the argument further. Freedom, he argued, was not freedom to do whatever one wanted, but freedom to pursue some good object and to do so in association with others rather than as an isolated or irresponsible individual.

The problem which arose with the extension of the electorate caused a rethinking of liberal conceptions of citizenship, in its actual as much as in its ideal form. Conservatives had always argued that democracy meant handing power to those who had neither the skill nor the altruism to use it wisely. The insistence on freedom as providing the conditions for individual growth, and not merely individual acquisition, went some way to answer this charge. By exercising political freedom, argued John Stuart Mill, people learnt how better to employ it. The motive for the proper use of freedom might be a self-interest more or less long sighted, rather than altruism or a sense of public duty. But since not all uses of freedom were proper, or not all actions could be described as truly in pursuit of freedom, wisdom and experience needed to be carefully cultivated.

Liberalism and collectivism

In the nineteenth century the gradual extension of the right to vote had led liberalism to reassess its direction. By the beginning of the twentieth century the vote was still only available for a minority of the adult population: no women had the vote, and only around 60 per cent of men. Even so the assumption that 'people' meant men, and that women were somehow no more than social and domestic auxiliaries, was sufficiently powerful for it to be assumed that democracy had been more or less achieved. A new challenge to liberalism was now provided by the massive extension of state collectivism, ostensibly under democratic authority. The problem of the material deprivation which sat uneasily with the formal, political equality which democracy promised, was tackled by liberalism through a revision of its attitudes towards government. The spread of democracy and the extension of the powers of the state were parallel and interwoven developments. The second seemed to offer a solution to the problems caused by the first. So-called 'new liberals' such as the sociologist L. T. Hobhouse responded with a redescription of the state as the appropriate agent for creating the material conditions in which individuals could pursue their own ends and realise their own potential as fully and as equally as possible.

Whilst the state was still undeniably in the hands of a privileged minority, liberalism could argue for political reform, economic restraint and personal liberties. The extension of the franchise by the reforms of 1832, 1867 and 1884 created a problem, for if the state arose out of the rational choices of all its subjects (or at least the majority of its male ones), did this alter in any way the need to insist on the rights of those subjects against it?

If a democratic state was different, as L. T. Hobhouse insisted that it was, then clearly it was not threatening in the way that an aristocratic state had been. Since the state was now the expression of the people's choice, rigidly to set limits to anything novel the state tried to do was to attempt to protect voters against themselves. The advance of new sections of the population into electoral citizenship drew attention to the ways in which large numbers of people did not have access to the kinds of resources traditionally if often unthinkingly associated with the liberal individual: education, leisure, capital, health. So by the beginning of the twentieth century restrictions on individual liberty had come to include, for 'new liberals' such as Hobhouse and J. A. Hobson, restricted access to the resources for self-determination, and it was being argued that public power, the state, had a vital role to play in providing training and education, health, housing, or the capital and raw materials which were necessary for production.

But that was not the only liberal response. For if the objection to the way property and its advantages were actually distributed stemmed from a liberal belief in its advantages for all, then it was equally plausible to argue that the expectation should be fulfilled. If the state had a part to play in this version, it was only as a brief or occasional redistributor of wealth, rather than as a permanent administrator of the nation's economic resources. This proposal of a once and for all redistribution was the solution advanced by Hilaire Belloc with his advocacy of 'distributism'.

But the attempt to develop a role for the collectivist state in the promotion of the individual's opportunities for economic and social development caused the beginnings of a fragmentation of liberalism which was to become a full scale diaspora in the twentieth century. In arguing for a 'new' liberalism, writers such as Hobhouse drew attention to developments or to a fear of them which had already led to a reassertion of more ancient liberal suspicions of government as inherently 'tory'.

In responding in this way, liberals caused some of their number to take a very different position, reasserting with new resolution the old suspicions that common moral purposes or state interference were both equally threats to liberty. Well before the development of the 'new liberalism' Herbert Spencer was warning of a slippery slope of well-meaning but misguided social reform which was leading to a 'new slavery' a 'new toryism'. Spencer's account of the development of nineteenth century history was of a damaging departure from the true principles of liberalism.

It was Spencer's reaction which, despite the fading reputation of its author, was to give direction to an increasingly powerful strand of twentieth century liberalism. What did not survive beyond Spencer was the comprehensiveness of the liberal denunciation of the regulation of individuals. For Spencer military and imperial activity, interference with religion or culture, taxation and economic regulation were all of a piece. That unity did not survive into the twentieth century. Two principal problems had to be addressed: property and government. Increasingly liberalism divided, with some applying its principles to one area, some to the other.

Both Spencer and Hobhouse had presented versions of liberalism which, though very different, aspired to be comprehensive. It was after Hobhouse, and after the end of the First World War, that liberalism began to fragment. For although Hobhouse advocated functions for the state which would have appalled Spencer, his conception of liberty remained a comprehensive one, enveloping all aspects of the person's life: domestic, political, cultural, moral, political, legal and economic. But the circumstances in which liberal, as all other, political thought developed, changed rapidly. The state, expanding its powers during the First World War, during the years of depression and unemployment leading up to the Second World War, and in the years of social democratic expansion of the first majority Labour government from 1945 to 1951, created a form of collectivism to which liberal ideas were applied in different, and diverging, directions.

There are four principal strands of liberalism in the twentieth century. The first continues with the collectivism, but with little else, of Hobhouse and leads to the finance state of Keynes – it remains sympathetic to economic collectivism, but retains the cultural individualism of the nineteenth century inheritance. The economic responsibilities of government can most effectively be fulfilled not by direct intervention, management, or ownership, but by the financial controls of taxation and investment which enable government to regulate demand. The second takes Spencer's economics but marries them with an increasingly conservative, even tory, view of culture. The third retains, in an extreme form, the coherence of Spencer in a version of libertarianism, with freedom depicted as a seamless whole ranging from self-policing to a free market in heroin. The fourth strand concerns itself with constitutional reform. It assumes that political structures can be improved without committing them to any particular social or economic outcomes, but that this can only be done by making the constitution both more open and more accessible to democratic influence.

Hobhouse was not the last liberal to have Liberal connections. Keynes argued that the Liberal Party provided the most appropriate instrument for achieving his blend of collectivism and capitalism, whilst the man who provided one of the most powerful rationales for the welfare state as it developed after the end of the Second World War in 1945, William Beveridge, argued for liberal policies and stood as a Liberal candidate for Parliament. But though they both gave the authority of their arguments to

Liberal Party politics, there was no reciprocal benefit for the influence of their ideas. The considerable and lasting influence which Keynes achieved over economic, and Beveridge over social, thought and policy was gained despite or without reference to their party allegiance. In one sense it was the more powerful for that. Without a strong party connection, their views were able to permeate where partisan resistance might otherwise have excluded them.

Liberalism, in lacking a powerful political vehicle of the kind which the Labour and Conservative parties provided for its rivals, developed less coherently, though with greater variety than they did, and emerged in unexpected places. One of the most interesting pieces of liberal political writing after the First World War was free from any party liaison. Harold Laski's argument on sovereignty fell squarely in the liberal tradition, in that it treated the state as both artificial and instrumental, and sought to demystify its operations by a functional dispersal of its most mysterious aspect: sovereignty. John Maynard Keynes, though frequently described as a liberal, was far more of a semi-detached intellectual.

By the second half of the century it was difficult to find expositions of liberalism in the traditional sense. There was though a growth of liberal speculation amongst political philosophers, whilst liberal ideas, though not liberal thinkers, proliferated amongst the ranks of socialists and conservatives. This marks liberalism off from socialism and from conservatism. Whilst conservatism in particular was relatively immune to international currents in political thought, liberalism, as it flourished within professional political theory in the universities, became increasingly a British instance of an international discussion.

III Society

Liberals have a conception of the individual, and a conception of the state. They are less well equipped to deal with anything in between, whether it be society as a whole, or the various groups and associations of which individuals may be members. They have been averse to attributing a role, other than a potentially oppressive one, to associations and groups larger than the individual but smaller than the nation. The choices which are available for explaining human social relations are consequently limited, for they must be either the result of the free rational choices of individuals co-operating with one another, or of the legal framework set by government. Thus Herbert Spencer argued that there were two principles on which social organisation could be based: voluntary co-operation for mutual advantage, which he termed the 'industrial' principle, or the 'militant' organisation of commands backed up by force. Certainly any other notion, of a society held together by convention, or custom, or expressive of some 'natural' human characteristics broader than the individual, sat uneasily with liberal understandings.

Yet liberalism required some understanding of human social behaviour since it was not credible to assume that every action was the result of fresh rational reflection. Either nature or convention had to be employed to fill the gap, and they frequently did so implicitly rather than explicitly.

Public life, private household

Because liberals have seen the principal division as one between free individual life and collective, state, coercion, they have associated freedom with the absence of legal restraint. Conversely, if individual conduct does not evidently arise from the exercise or threat of such restraint, liberals have generally assumed it to arise from free choice. But at the same time there is a division, both within society and within the life of individuals, between public and private. And it was assumed not only that the character of co-operation in the public sphere would take place within certain natural limits, and on the basis of certain natural distributions of human nature, but that those natural characteristics would almost entirely explain how people lived their lives in the private, domestic sphere. John Stuart Mill, like Spencer and others liberal and non-liberal alike, took it for granted that in the distribution of responsibilities within the household, the task of nurture and upbringing would be taken up by women. This caused feminists to criticise both thinkers like Mill for their assumptions about the division of responsibilities between the sexes, and liberalism for halting its liberating insistence on rights at the gates of some of the most flagrant institutionalisations of their infringement.

When liberals applied their beliefs to the institution of marriage, they did so in a way which illustrated the ambivalence of liberal assumptions. On the one hand were those like Mill who sought to reform the law in such a way as to equalise the treatment of men and women; on the other libertarians who considered that the only justification which law had for concerning itself with marriage at all was in order to secure the well-being of children. But both liberals and libertarians assumed that the end was the maximisation of individual choice, and that the only restraints on that choice were law and nature.

With the fragmentation of liberalism in the twentieth century, different assumptions were made. Whilst there were still those, such as Samuel Brittan, who argued an across-the-board liberalism from capital to conduct, the most prominent liberal writer of the second half of the twentieth century, F. A. Hayek, took a very different view from Mill of the character and context of individual choice in cultural and moral matters. But even when convention, an apparently conservative rather than liberal notion, was employed as it was by Hayek in the second half of the twentieth century, it was employed in a liberal manner. For Hayek conventions or traditions were external to the individual who had to take them into account when shaping his actions. For a conservative, on the other hand, the very individual who chose was a product of tradition – the traditions existed as powerfully within the individual as they did around him.

Liberalism and eccentricity

The idea that society is natural whilst government is artificial does not necessarily constitute a simple and straightforward confirmation of convention. It can provide, on the contrary, an effective case for the most diverse forms of individual conduct.

For if society and the life of people unconstrained by government are natural, then there are no criteria by which they may be judged other than by the observation of what in fact exists. No belief or manner of life can be ruled out, and the grounds for criticising the conduct of other people can only be that the ways in which they pursue their objectives – though not necessarily the objectives themselves – cause harm to others. Liberals have not been merely indifferent to the varieties of human conduct, however, but have frequently applauded them as a source of vigour and progress in society. Thus John Stuart Mill argued in 1859 that 'the amount of eccentricity in a society has generally been proportional to the amount of genius, mental vigour, and moral courage it contained.'[3] One hundred years later, although with many massive reservations, F. A. Hayek dedicated his *The Constitution of Liberty* to 'the unknown civilisation that is growing in America'.[4] It was precisely this aspect of liberalism which has so distressed conservatives. T. S. Eliot complained that liberalism was merely corrosive, Roger Scruton that it always dissolved, never created.[5] The so-called 'permissive' legislation of the 1960s was liberal in character, and supported by liberal arguments. Thus when in the 1960s there began a long and continuing debate over abortion, it was appropriate that it was a Liberal backbencher, David Steel, whose private member's bill led to a change in the law to allow women greater access to the medical termination of pregnancy. The principal argument in favour of the maximum individual freedom has always been a liberal one, and has rested on the double base of an appeal to individual rights and to social benefit.

Religion

Liberalism was indifferent to religion. But individual liberals often held strong religious beliefs, and in the nineteenth century religion was a subject of major concern for liberals. Unlike conservatives, for whom religion was both a central thread in the national life and a proper concern of the state, liberals viewed religion as important only in so far as it might be a matter of individual conviction or persuasion. What mattered was the right of individuals to practise what religion they chose; but it did not matter whether or not religion was practised. When liberalism and religious belief kept company, it was the more individualist and anti-authoritarian forms of Protestantism that were most common. Liberalism has been agnostic rather than atheist, and hence as tolerant of belief as of scepticism. One of the policies pursued by parliamentary Liberalism was thus the separation of church and state, at least in Wales where the status of the Anglican Church as the established church could be criticised as the use of state power to impose on the population a form of religion to which the majority of them did not subscribe. It was a Liberal government, that of H. H. Asquith, which in 1914, finally passed legislation dis-establishing the Church of Wales.

Liberal interest in religion did not survive the inroads made against officially and legally supported religious discrimination, which was itself in part a matter of the advance of toleration, but in part also a consequence of the decline of religion itself after the First World War.

IV Economy

Property lay at the heart of liberalism, which is in the first place an economic doctrine, or rather a doctrine about economics. Liberalism begins not so much with the individual as with the individual's right over material objects and his own person. The rights which individuals were believed to possess could all be seen as rights of property: over inanimate objects and materials, and over themselves, what has been termed 'possessive indivi-dualism'.[6] Political and social freedom was the right to self-ownership. Liberal individuals, in other words, exercised their individuality by their property relationships. Property was the circle which they drew around themselves, within which they exercised a freedom which the state should not interfere with but, on the contrary, which it had a duty to protect.

Whilst it would be wrong to see nineteenth century liberalism as espousing pure laissez-faire or free trade, or to assume that a qualified form of those policies was not advocated by conservatives as well, the arguments in favour of such economic arrangements were essentially liberal ones. An advocacy of the greatest possible freedom in the ownership and use of property formed a central part of the rhetoric of parliamentary Liberalism in the nineteenth century, from Cobden and Bright through to Gladstone. When, at the beginning of the twentieth century, the academic lawyer A. V. Dicey attacked what he saw as the 'tide of collectivism', the most threatening current seemed to him to be the various infringements which the state had made of the untrammelled rights of property, whether by straightforward taxation, or by regulations on the use of land, factories or raw materials.[7]

The nature of property had been transformed by the end of the nineteenth century. Two changes were fundamental: a shift from agriculture to industry, and the development through limited liability of a far greater separation between the ownership of a business enterprise, and participation in or even familiarity with what that enterprise actually did. It had previously been possible to imagine economic reforms which would place greater control in the hands of ordinary workers, uniting production and ownership. In theory a rural proletariat could be replaced by a land-owning peasantry. The factory worker could with far less plausibility be replaced by the craftsman or the self-governing co-operative. The collectivisation of production in factories meant that even a myth of ownership for the majority of the population in the materials of their daily work became unconvincing. Some form of public agency, which meant the state either locally or nationally, acquired in these circumstances a new and enlarged function.

Whilst liberals have seen individual action as the motive of economic life, they have always accorded government a role in allowing that motive fullest play. That has not necessarily meant a minimum state which simply sets and enforces rules of fair play. Liberals from Hobhouse to Keynes have argued that there are factors affecting the free economic activity of individuals which lie outside their control but which yet are not the result of the actions of government. Accidental concentrations of wealth, restrictions on economic information, accidents of birth or fortune which incapacitate some and confer advantages on others, all these can and should be remedied by government, but in such a way as to enhance rather than to replace individual initiative. The most passionate use of class politics in the twentieth century was not by a socialist, but by the Liberal Chancellor of the Exchequer David Lloyd George in 1909–10 in his attacks on the landed aristocracy as the possessors of a privilege which denied economic freedoms to others, and which must be ended by the introduction of a tax on land. The land campaign had a long radical tradition stretching back into the 1870s. For whilst liberalism advocated the greatest freedoms in the use of property, it could also argue that this involved a prior freedom in the opportunities of gaining access to property. Land, being finite, unlike all other forms of capital, was a special case.

However much the state might involve itself with economic activity, it could never do more than provide a context or facilitate a direction. It could never provide the motive springs of economic activity, which lay in the free and rational activity of the individual. But within those limits, a very wide variety of liberal economic proposals were possible, from Spencer's minimal state and survival of the fittest, to Keynes's demand management by a state which involved itself in a market economy in order not to supersede but to cultivate it. Hence Keynes's proposals for demand management, though they used the apparently socialist instrument of state economic power, did so in pursuit of the facilitation of individual demands and purchasing decisions which were unpredictable save in their general volume. Just so had Hobhouse argued for public ownership as the instrument achieving the maximum possible distribution of private ownership.

Although liberalism is normally associated with 'classical laissez-faire' and the unconstrained individual pursuit of profit, mere materialism has always been the subject of critical qualification, in terms both of its individual and of its social consequences. This concern with the consequences and character of individual choice has enabled the liberal strands in twentieth century political argument to run in two quite distinct directions. The strand of liberalism which runs from L. T. Hobhouse on into the twentieth century sees freedom being exercised most fully not simply when it is unconstrained, but when it has facilities for giving effect to choices: health, education, property or capital. This meant that the state acted as the great facilitator, and fed into the argument, in the 1980s, that markets could only operate either effectively or fairly in conjunction with some form of socialism. The strand of liberalism which ran from Spencer, on the other hand, led into a renewed celebration of market capitalism and minimally constrained or regulated private ownership as the most effective condition for free and varied individual life. As liberalism fragmented, the first strand was most frequently found in the argument of market socialists, the second, with the exception of writers such as Samuel Brittan and the 'anarcho-capitalist' libertarians, in the company of arguments which, like those of F. A. Hayek, were socially, culturally and morally deeply conservative.

V State and Politics

The language of rights is a characteristically liberal one, rooted as it is in a conception of the individual as the starting point for any moral analysis of human life. The individual is prior to the state in liberal theory from Locke through Paine to Mill and Hobhouse. Government arises to serve the needs of individuals living in society, and its authority arises from their consent, an idea frequently expressed in terms of a hypothetical 'contract' made either between rulers and ruled, or among the citizens themselves. Even when liberals could observe, as did Paine, that in historical fact many governments, including that of England, had arisen 'out of a conquest', that did not alter their view of individual consent as the only proper basis on which it could be justified.[8]

But at the same time liberals like Mill argued that politics was the most 'enlarged' level at which people could exercise their facilities, the one where they most fully transcended the mundane and the particular. There is in other words not an inconsistency, but a tension, within liberalism, between the view that the individual life is the sphere within which freedom and the fullest use of human talents is exercised, and the view that those talents can only be fully exercised when a perspective limited to the concerns and experience of the individual is transcended. The individual is both citizen, exercising powers, and subject enjoying rights. As liberalism responded to the implications of its commitment to democracy, the theory of active citizenship gained in importance.

Because liberalism both accepts government as a necessary and useful activity, and has clear views about the threats which government has posed and can pose and how they should be countered and limited, arguments about the state and the constitution have always been close to its heart. And because for liberals the institutions of government are human creations, they are subject to rational appraisal and reconstruction. Whilst conservatives have seen in the institutions of government the distillation of the wisdom of history, and socialists the biases of a class society or the neutral instrument for the expression of the people's choices, neither party has been in a position to accord importance to government as a system of political power *per se*, and in consequence has not considered, though for very different reasons, that constitutional reform was a matter of importance. For liberals, on the other hand, constitutional arrangements are both appropriate for radical review, and the potential cause of major flaws in the life of the community.

Because for liberals government was a means to other ends, liberalism has taken seriously the possible choices about the manner of conducting government and politics. Discussion of alternative methods of electing public representatives formed a central part of John Stuart Mill's *Essay on Representative Government*. Liberalism has been associated with demands for the extension and reform of voting, and for the extension of the right to vote to all regardless of sex, on the grounds of individual rights. Because liberalism has always had a constitutional dimension, it has never been adequately described as a belief simply about the extent of government. Government for liberals has three related qualities: its extent, its distribution, and its manner.

So at the end of the nineteenth century it was Dicey who gave a liberal account of a constitution which took second place to individual liberties rooted in individual property ownership, and which was checked by the sense of liberty and justice of its subjects. England, unlike the nations of continental Europe, knew nothing of states with privileges over and above the law which governed ordinary subjects. In such a relationship the state was essential, as the recogniser and defender of rights, but secondary, in that it was neither the creator nor the source of those rights. At the beginning of the twentieth century the legal theorist and historian F. W. Maitland described a state which recognised and acknowledged, but in no way created, the social identities of the corporations which composed the society which it governed. At the end of the First World War Harold Laski sought to dissolve the mysteries of sovereignty into the more mundane and tangible rights of the groups and associations which formed the social life of subjects. In all these instances, a liberal theory of government denied any priority to the state, and sought constantly to check the state's ambitions by subordinating them to the prior purposes of citizens.

Liberalism has been a source of the widest proposals for constitutional reform. If the political community is one of citizens freely contracting with a government which their wills authorise, then there is nothing immutable about the extent or character of that community. If the inhabitants of Ireland, or of Wales, or of Scotland, wish to be governed not from London but from Dublin, Cardiff, or Edinburgh, there is no answer to their claims in reference to either law or tradition. But neither, paradoxically, is there any ground for questioning the assertion by a group of people that they are a nation. The cultural roots of nationality lie in the same realm of the acceptedly 'natural' as do the divisions between members of the patriarchal family.

It was Liberal politicians and Liberal governments who between 1885 and 1921 wrestled with a series of solutions to the Irish demand first for home rule and then for independence, just as it was Liberals like Lloyd George who in the first quarter of the present century flew the kite of regional assemblies for other portions of the United Kingdom, and in particular for Wales. In the 1970s the idea of 'community politics', an attempt to reinvigorate local government and politics by enhancing the extent and quality of local citizen activity, was characteristically both a liberal conception and an original contribution to public life of Liberal politics.

Liberal belief in the fundamental value of individually determined courses of action, scepticism towards government, and preference for voluntary and commercial, over legislative, forms of organisation, had an international corollary. For liberal politicians such as Cobden or Bright in the nineteenth century, liberalism as a theory of 'negative' liberty in economic and political relations applied equally to the relations between states. Aristocracy was opposed at home, and imperialism abroad. Spencer saw the link, and at the start of the twentieth century Norman Angel asserted the pacific consequences of increasing international trade and economic exchange. This belief in the possibility of modestly rational international relations distinguished liberalism from socialist sceptical attribution of sinister economic interests at work in the relations of states, and conservative insistence on a vigorous assertion of national security. If it was an optimism that was regularly disappointed in the twentieth century, it was at the same time one that was never extinguished. When in the 1950s there was talk of an 'end of ideology', and a domestic politics of small negotiations, and in the 1990s of an 'end of history' and a civilised, commercial, relationship between states following the abdication of communist autocracies, the continuing vitality of liberal hopes was very clear.

VI Trailer

The realignments of the various strands of liberalism in the twentieth century meant that whilst economic liberalism allied itself with strands of conservatism in the 'New Right', political and social liberalism was found in conjunction with the arguments of market socialism and the movement for constitutional reform. The decline of party Liberalism, and the continuing vitality of academic liberalism, gave liberal ideas in the closing decades of the twentieth century an easy and effective access that was denied to both socialism and conservatism.

4

SOCIALISM

I Introduction

Socialism has had many homelands, all of which it has at one time or another denied. Russia, Spain, Yugoslavia, Sweden, Cuba have all been both awarded the accolade of working futures, and dismissed as frauds or failures with as much vehemence as ever was directed against mere enemies. At home, however, socialism has found few good examples. Hope has generally lain in the future, and socialists have found few domestic precedents for their ideals. Conservatives by contrast have had few countries which either they or any one else have acknowledged as conservative homelands, whilst being ever ready with foreign examples of how enterprise and ambition are set properly to work in more entrepreneurial nations. At home, in contrast to socialism, conservatism has justified its proposals by claiming that they follow the predominant contours of the nation's life.

Yet socialism in Britain has not been entirely without domestic examples for its proposals. One of its subordinate themes has been the claim that the principles of socialism can already be detected in the qualities of ordinary people, or in the institutions which the people have themselves established. For Robert Blatchford at the end of the nineteenth century and for George Orwell in the years between the two world wars, it was the ruling class who were alien, whilst the general body of citizens already possessed the basic human materials for a good society. For the New Left writers of the 1960s and 1970s it was in the collective solidarity of the trade union and co-operative movements that the true sturdy oak of British traditions was to be discovered.[1]

Socialism has in general given first place to arguments that things should be and could be done differently and better, not just by small amendments or reforms, but by the application of new principles. It has been characterised by enormous variety, but a pervasive characteristic has been an assertion of the social against, though not to the exclusion of, the individual. The starting point for socialist analysis, and sometimes, but not always, for identifying the principles which should determine the distribution of goods and services, benefits and powers, is society rather than the individual. Wealth is believed to be an essentially social product, in that without the economic context which is greater than and distinct from individual contribution, economic activity could never take place at all.

In seeking to explain why, given the social nature of production, its rewards are so unsocially distributed, socialists have identified a variety of causes. The principal ones have been self-interest and irrationality. The existing system which places the means of production in private hands is an example of self-interest using its advantages to exploit the majority in the interests of a propertied minority. Alternatively, the chaos or anarchy of markets is evidence of the limited rationality of those who, both in their own interests and in everybody else's, ought to agree to ways of arranging things which were both more just and more efficient.

Like conservatism, socialism is a doctrine of order. It differs however in the means whereby it expects order to be achieved or maintained: by the triumph of reason over chaos, and of co-operation over conflict. Socialists have generally supposed that there are self-evident or discoverable principles of justice whereby goods and services can be made available, and that some kind of public system of social services will be an effective and accountable mechanism for achieving this just distribution. Like conservatism too, socialism has had its analogies with religion. But whereas conservatism gave to government the role of a secular priesthood, shepherding a flawed humanity with a firm but paternal hand, socialism has at times been millenarian and utopian, with an egalitarianism which is the political equivalent of the priesthood of all believers and of the puritan suspicion of bishops and kings.

Of the three ideals of liberty, equality and fraternity inherited by socialists from the French Revolution, equality was the most important. But whilst the principle of equality was not derived from reflection on British conditions, its application frequently was. Socialism was always articulated within the domestic context of Britain, and its standards were commonly, though not exclusively, taken from those of the more fortunate. Equality meant not so much an unrecognisably transformed social order, as one in which benefits currently enjoyed by a few, were dispersed equally amongst all. So whilst conservatism responded to challenges and liberalism to restrictions, socialism responded to unfairness, inadequacies, deficiencies and deprivations.

Liberty, in socialist writing, frequently appears as freedom from hunger, or ill health, or unemployment, rather than as the unpredictable action of self-governing individuals. Neither has it generally had a strong political face, not because socialists have been indifferent to political liberty, but because political liberty has not generally been considered by socialists to be in any serious way impaired in Britain. Lacking either the liberal theory of politics as a distinctive activity, or the liberal wariness towards government, socialists have tended to see the state as merely a blank page on which the electorate's wishes can be written.

II Historical Setting

Whereas conservatism has reacted to challenges from outside and to threats from below, and liberalism to domestic political constrictions, socialism has been doubly motivated by domestic deprivation on the one hand, and by examples of more promising practice both at home and abroad and in the speculations of utopians on the other. There has thus been an overlap between the historical circumstances in which liberalism and socialism have developed: industrialism and poverty in the nineteenth century, recession, depression, unemployment and inequality in the twentieth.

There have been five principal phases in the history of socialist thought. First, an early socialism which extended ideals drawn in part from the French Revolution to proposals for a more just organisation of an industrial society. Second, from the 1880s onwards, a socialism which was united in being directed specifically against capitalism, but divided between utopians, evangelists, and collectivist reformers. Third, from the period after the First World War until the beginning of the second half of the twentieth century, a socialism which was democratic in method and optimistically collectivist in policies and expectations. Fourth, from the mid 1950s until the end of the 1970s, an attempt to extend socialist ideals beyond conceptions of simple economic class, and to discover ways of dispersing power in all its forms. Fifth and finally, and in response to the arguments of the New Right, a redefinition of both socialism and liberty in a way which emphasised the maximisation of individual choice in some form of market.

Early socialism

Socialism is one of the principal heirs of the French revolutionary commitment to liberty, equality and fraternity. But the lines of succession are neither simple, straightforward, nor unmixed. Early writers to whom the title 'socialist' is applied set forward arguments which, whilst they were intended to benefit the workers in the new urban industrial forms of production, gave those workers no special place in the path from an unsatisfactory present to a desirable future. In the proposals of Robert Owen for a system of exchange based on labour, the 'landholder and capitalist would be benefited by this arrangement in the same degree with the labourer'.[2] To that extent the early socialists were utopians with a vision for society as a whole. The special relationship with the working class came later.

'Modern' Socialism

What is normally thought of as socialism did not emerge until the 1880s, and was in general seen as involving a very particular relationship to the industrial working class. The second wave of socialists from the 1880s onwards though still thinking in terms of the entire community, nonetheless also saw their arguments as having a particular relevance to the position of industrial workers. Industrial workers were the class associated with the innovative production of industrialism and, being urban, the most visibly exploited by existing arrangements. In continental Europe this linkage in political thought of socialism with the working class arose from Marxism, but in Britain in the nineteenth century it came just as much from a supposition about who had most to gain by an attack on capitalism, who were the most likely allies in the construction of a new order, and who were, at the time, most obviously excluded from the full benefits of citizenship. Whether or not the relationship between socialism and the working class was necessary or merely contingent, it was to be a potentially weak association which by the end of the twentieth century had developed into a massive theoretical fault line.

Socialism in the last quarter of the nineteenth century was developing at a time when liberalism had already begun to believe that democracy had exorcised toryism and aristocracy from the state, and to see government as a vehicle for popular politics, or even for the pursuit of the reform of the condition of the people. The ambitions of late nineteenth and early twentieth century socialists did little more than extend this liberal programme. What was envisaged was a beneficent socialist state, purged certainly of much of its coercive trappings, but nonetheless busily ubiquitous in ensuring the material well-being of its subjects. Such a socialism was, argued the Fabian essayists in 1889, no more than the logical development of democracy and even, argued one of them, the essential condition for the full achievement of individualism.[3]

Although there were differences on other grounds between pragmatic collectivists and the more visionary evangelists of socialism, in the matter of government they were united, if only by default. For Fabian Socialists like Beatrice and Sidney Webb, the extension of the responsibilities of the state was no more than the common sense encouragement of a well-established process whereby a society which was increasingly democratic took greater and greater control over the efficient conduct of its own affairs. For socialist publicists like James Ramsay MacDonald or James Keir Hardie, greater state control over the economy and greater state provision for the material and intellectual welfare of the population raised few fears of excessive local or central power, since that power was seen principally as a mere instrument in the hands of either objective experts or an increasingly informed electorate. The state was no more than the translucent instrument of justice in either a transformed society freed from greed, or a fair society which gave each their just share. Beatrice and Sidney Webb thought that much of what was to be done under socialism would hardly be government at all in the conventional sense: 'the government of men must be distinguished from the administration of things.'[4]

But the optimism of socialist collectivists was located in the context of a far more pervasive nineteenth century assumption, shared with liberals and even some conservatives, that the direction of human history in general, and of European history in particular, was towards higher and higher levels of material and cultural civilisation. This assumption facilitated the very different expectations of those socialist utopians such as Edward Carpenter or William Morris for whom the future promised a society which had very little if any formal government, and where socialism meant altruistic co-operation and the pleasures of the simple productive life, rather than the rational administration of the social democratic state.

Democratic socialism

The third phase of socialism was a social democratic theory learnt in the experience of electoral politics and Labour governments on the one hand, and confirmed by the experience of increasingly non-democratic methods in the Soviet Union on the other. Although the principles of socialism could be derived from the French Revolution, and its image of insurrection has always derived as much from Paris as from Moscow or St Petersburg, its foreign examples of positive policy were taken, in the first instance, from twentieth century revolutions. The overwhelming tone of British socialism has been democratic. Its attitude towards the Russian Revolution of 1917, and towards the system that was subsequently established, was thus increasingly critical. What attracted admiration was the apparent success of the soviets in replacing a system based on the private ownership of capital with one where economic resources were both planned and publicly owned. Depression and unemployment were seen to be avoided, whilst resources were directed towards the provision, partly through public services, of minimum standards of living for the mass of the population. What repelled was the concentration of political power and its oppressive and murderous use.

Seemingly dramatic political events often proved the most inspiring or illuminating for socialists. Revolutionary transformations abroad could excite and inspire, whilst socialism often found its most compelling domestic examples in the activities of government in wartime. The First World War provided examples of swift extensions of government power into the control of production and manpower. And if people could be conscripted in the interests of war, then capital could be conscripted in the interests of peace. The years from 1918 to 1939 saw mounting unemployment at a time when whatever the increasing evident blemishes of the new Soviet state, it appeared to be able to use collectivist economic planning to ensure the employment and the living standards of its population. So socialists responded to the failures of indigenous systems by proposing their amendment or replacement, particularly where the consequences of inefficiency fell upon the living standards of the working class. With the election victory of 1945 and the establishment of the first majority Labour government under Clement Attlee, the possibilities of democratic socialism seemed confirmed just at the time when the totalitarian character of state socialism in eastern Europe was becoming widely apparent.

The experience of Russia enhanced the constitutional awareness of socialists, and made even firmer an almost conservative
adherence to parliamentary democracy. The years which for
some confirmed the validity of this constitutional rectitude, also
provided a milestone in the socialist conception of both the aims
of socialism and the constitutional and political forms to which it
should aspire. Six years of majority Labour government were
able to achieve a massive extension of public ownership and of
publicly provided social services. But they seemed to many to
have made less change in the control which ordinary citizens
exercised over their lives, or in the general pattern of power with
society. Nationalisation may have transferred major industries
and services into the ownership of 'the people', but it seemed to
make little difference to the day to day lives of those people as
workers or the users of services. Why is it, asked Brian Abel-
Smith in 1958, that in the welfare state, whilst the customer is
always right, the citizen is 'usually wrong'?[5]

Revisionism and the New Left

In so far as British socialism has been parliamentary and non-
indeed anti-, revolutionary, its course has followed that of parliamentary politics. Even its more radical moments have been in
response to the apparent failures or stagnations of the parliamentary stream. Both the 'revisionism' of the 1950s and the
'New Left' of the 1960s and 1970s arose in circumstances where
the original parliamentary optimisms seemed either fulfilled or
exhausted. The very successes of the Attlee government of 1945–
51 left a feeling of incompleteness. So much and yet so little
seemed to have changed

The years between 1951 and the early 1970s thus saw both a
broadening of socialist argument beyond the categories of economic class, and a concern with political arrangements, with
decentralisation, with 'community power', and with various
forms of workers' control. On the one hand so-called revisionists
argued, with Anthony Crosland, that public ownership was a
means not an end, and not the most effective means either.
Increasing educational opportunity, egalitarian taxation, and

Keynesian finance would achieve far more than direct nationalisation. Equality was the goal, but it was as much a matter of social status and of power, as of material standards of living. On the other hand the coalition of anarchists, feminists and decentralising socialists who composed the New Left pointed out that equality of power required political and social arrangements which radically redistributed power away from centralised governmental and political organisations, as well as away from capitalism and patriarchy.

Socialism and the New Right

A dramatic change came after 1979 when, with the election of a radical Conservative government, socialists for the first time became people not only with much to gain but with a great deal to lose. The so-called 'Thatcherite' or 'New Right' assault on the principles of universal social services and publicly owned utilities, combined with the drive to place all forms of provision of goods and services on a market/cash basis placed socialism on the defensive. Not until the end of the 1980s did a renewed definition of socialism take place, which gave a revived and restated place to liberty, both political and economic. Socialism had always drawn on international examples, if not international writings, for its political thought. By the time it developed its response to the New Right, not only was it engaging with a body of political and economic doctrines which were themselves international as much as simply British, but its own network of reference, which was traditionally a wide one, had broadened even further as British political thought itself became more and more part of an international debate.

III Society

For the early socialists capitalist society was characterised by injustice, inequality and oppression. A socialist society would thus be a transformed society, and social relations would be governed by co-operation and altruism rather than by competition and greed. Socialism meant a new life, and socialist citizens would be different from the citizens of capitalism. For some the transformation was radical, and involved semi-utopian intentions and experiments, from Robert Owen's model industrial town at New Lanark through Carpenter's peasant-sized agricultural household in Yorkshire to the communes of the 1960s. But the alternative socialist conception was of changes which were centred on the world of paid employment and formal politics, with the 'private' sphere left properly alone. The Fabian Socialists very firmly proclaimed that socialism had nothing to say on the family, religion, or any other such matters. The implication of having no policy towards this 'private' sphere was that in general the assumptions made by those who eschewed experimentation were thoroughly conventional and patriarchal. This did not prevent such 'a-social' socialism from being on occasion utopian or visionary. But the fraternity that was attributed to such utopias was most obviously a solidarity at the non-domestic workplace, and hence principally amongst males. The images of utopia (or at least of eutopia, as practical and realisable imaginative schemes were termed by the town-planner Patrick Geddes), were male, industrial and fraternal. They were neither domestic nor female. Even the egalitarian utopia described by William Morris in *News from Nowhere*, whilst it appears to have moved away from the patriarchal family, still has the women hovering around the fringes of the action, waiting on the tables of male conversation.

The enthusiasm for socialism as transformation led some to attribute to their expectations the kind of qualities normally associated with religion, and indeed to talk of the religion or, as Keir Hardie put it, 'the glorious Gospel' of socialism.[6] The use of religious motifs drew on the non-conformist culture in which late Victorian and Edwardian socialism flourished. But it reflected also the need to find some basis for the altered social character which a socialist society would need. If co-operation was to succeed self-seeking and conflict, some different ethos would be required, some different motive for social interaction. If religion could save souls, perhaps a secular religion could save societies.

Religion had a second contribution to make to socialist argument. Not only was a co-operative or altruistic motive required for individuals in a socialist society, but the general principles on which that society was to be based needed ethical justification. Religion could provide that, either in the appeals to charity and compassion in the 'socialist gospel' of James Keir Hardie, or in the egalitarian arguments of a Christian and socialist such as R. H. Tawney. The Christian view of all people as equally children of God provided for Tawney an obligation to begin with the presumption of equality in one's treatment of others, and to see fraternity as not just socially rewarding, but morally required. 'A Christianity which resigns the economic world to the devil appears to me, in short, not Christianity at all'.[7]

But there was another view of a socialist society. The values which would characterise it were not an aspiration towards which men and women should work, but a reality already in the lives of ordinary people. The tension was not between capitalist present and socialist future, so much as between the values and culture of ordinary people, and the forms of behaviour imposed on them by their political and economic rulers. For George Orwell writing about the unemployed of Lancashire in *The Road to Wigan Pier* this meant ordinary working class decency and fraternity. Orwell, who has often been dismissed by socialists for not being properly revolutionary, was remarkable for placing such a heavy emphasis upon class. It was not only for him the principal dimension of inequality – so was it for other socialists – but also the principal division between a culture that was solid, traditional, and rooted in national virtues, and one that was deracinated, displaced and corrupt: 'in all societies the common people must live to some extent *against* the existing order.'[8]

Orwell drew on indigenous examples, where his predecessors had tended to imagine the future, and his contemporaries to admire the East. For New Left writers in the 1960s and 1970s the existing decencies of the working class were given more academic form in the idea of a working class culture, frequently examined in the work of socialist historians. An attempt was made to base accounts of possible social progress on the existing values of collective working class organisation, but to do so in a way which treated them as a resource rather than as a blueprint.

Thus for writers like E. P. Thompson and Raymond Williams, there was the possibility of a socialism which was both radical and transformative, but grounded in British traditions rather than in either foreign example or abstract principle: 'Perhaps, without our knowledge, the key to change has been tossed into British hands, and the world waits impatiently upon us to turn the lock'.[9] But for the market socialists of the 1980s starting from existing foundations was to mean creating frameworks within which the aspirations of ordinary people, whatever and however varied they were, could be realised. In the version presented by Orwell, this had been not merely patriotic but, despite the distinction which he had drawn between defensive patriotism and aggressive nationalism, nationalist, in that it had involved the invocation of a cultural ideal, even though it was one located in existing rather than in hoped for practices and virtues. In its final version it was antithetical to nationalism, since markets are a means of justifying all wants and none. Socialist markets moreover both treat everyone as equal citizens, and can give no preferences or even recognition to cultural or national divisions.

Fraternity has been the ethos of equality, the mode of social conduct appropriate to a society not divided by privilege. Hence the place, always as a minor theme but always deeply embedded, within socialism of a cultural critique of commercial competitiveness, and the articulation of alternative forms of social organisation and alternative values: fraternity, co-operation, art. This minor but essential theme was to retain its place in socialism until challenged in the 1980s in the debate over markets and choice. Market socialists might insist on the importance of various forms of workers' control, but the freedom which markets promised was not necessarily compatible with any wider cultural community.

IV Economics

Socialism began as a belief that production was a social rather than an individual activity, and that thus collective rather than individual control, and collective rather than individual benefit, was the appropriate arrangement. There was a complementary suspicion of the individual pursuit of individual interests, and of the individual ownership of property. For much of the history of socialism in the United Kingdom, property was a term descriptive of something that was not just socially undesirable, but morally distasteful. Socialists were hostile both to the conservative notion of property as a privileged trust associated with exceptional qualities, and the liberal notion of property as the means to individual progress and satisfaction. The first offended egalitarianism, the second collectivism. When R. H. Tawney stigmatised contemporary society in 1920 as 'acquisitive' he was dismissing from the lofty high ground of moral certainty the very desire for material enrichment.[10] The obverse of this was a reluctance amongst socialists to take account of the material desires of those whom they championed, or to ask what was the qualitative or moral difference between the worker's desire for a dry roof or a back garden, and the bourgeois desire for double glazing or a patio.

Socialists have not generally shared the conservative view of the nobility of labour, though they have often believed in the nobility of labourers. There has been a distinction within socialism between those who saw work as a necessity rendered unpleasant by capitalist exploitation, which could be rendered less onerous under socialism, and those who saw work as potentially creative and satisfying, but prevented from being so because the workers were made into the objects of other people's control or exploitation. The first view led to public ownership, the second to workers' control.

It is the first strand which has been dominant, with a largely uncritical acceptance of bureaucracy and/or management. For the rejection of both conservative and liberal conceptions of property left socialists with little choice but some form of abstracted collective ownership, where nobody owned capital because everybody owned it. The problem was that however viable this might be as a principle, it was impossible to translate into practice. Somebody had to exercise the rights and powers of property, whatever the theories which were employed to justify their doing so. That somebody, for most socialists, and with very little reflection, was assumed to be the state. This had the consequence of adopting the substance of the conservative position, but replacing aristocracy with bureaucracy and management. The virtues of understanding and responsibility which tories had attached to the possession of broad acres, socialists transferred to the possession of broad qualifications.

The second view of work considered capitalism, and sometimes industrialism, as institutions which had perverted work from its proper creative function. In the writings of William Morris it led to the view that 'the reward of labour is life', and that it was perfectly possible to replace 'useless toil' by 'useful labour'.[11] But in so far as socialism was presented as an alternative to existing manners of doing things, it was also for some a transformation so complete as to render existing forms not only of work but of government unnecessary and inappropriate. The radical form of this was Morris's communist socialism. The reformist version consisted of arguments for workers' control and guild socialism, whereby producers organised and managed their own workshops and factories, but did so under the general co-ordinative supervision of a democratic state.

The difficulty with such a view was that it could imply something that was almost a form of workers' capitalism. Its vulnerability to criticism from more orthodox collectivists arose from its reluctance to grasp the nettle of property sufficiently firmly. For despite the rejection of capitalism associated with the various forms of workers' control, they all placed a central value on precisely that relationship between a worker and the material objects of his or her trade which property guaranteed. Unless advocates of workers' control thought through the implications of the paradox 'property is theft' – for to object to theft is to accept some form of property as valuable – they were vulnerable to the charge that anything less than control by society as a whole was less than democracy, and reproduced precisely the partisan and partial opposition between the interests of a few and the interests of everyone. Beatrice and Sidney Webb were able to bring just this charge against the early twentieth century exponents of workers' control, the guild socialists. The problem lay in the conceptualising of society, and it was difficult to see how this could be done save as the collectivity which embraced all its members. And it was in revolt against just such a dilemma that socialist pluralists such as G. D. H. Cole attempted to develop a theory of society which was not monolithically collectivist, and a theory of socialism which incorporated and nurtured variety.

Both forms of socialism involved assumptions about the nature of human beings and human society. But whereas the version which held optimistic assumptions about the state was less hopeful about ordinary humanity, those who were disinclined to give much of a role to government were the more hopeful about the possibilities for ungoverned, or less governed, human progress. The one was optimistic about rulers, politicians and experts, the other about ordinary people. It was the first form of socialism which predominated in the first half of the twentieth century, leading to an emphasis on public ownership and economic planning by public bodies. The emphasis of taxation policy, in so far as it was a device for the allocation of income, was as much on making the wealthy pay their share, as on maximising the disposable incomes of the poor.

One of the arguments developed within the movement lumped under the loose collective title 'New Left' from the early 1960s onward, was that there were resources for radical change in the organisations and institutions of people as they actually were. It was possible to reconcile pluralism and collectivism by making the latter an assertion on behalf of all against minority power, and the former a means of arranging life in a society freed of domination and orthodoxy. This socialist pluralism was feasible when the various social identities were seen to arise from either the different jobs people did or the different industries in which they did them. The overall coherence of a society structured, rather than divided, along distinctions of occupational class nonetheless held the whole enterprise together. It could not so readily assimilate or take account of quite different dimensions of social life, those of nationality, ethnicity or religion. And when it came to the divisions of gender, and those between the public and the private sphere, socialist pluralism had as little to say as did socialist collectivism.

V State and Politics

Socialists have shared the later liberal assumption that in a democracy the state is, at least potentially, a neutral institution which can reflect the wishes and aspirations of the people. There has also been a belief that such a social democratic state would be at one and the same time representative and expert. Fabianism of the Webbs or Shaw was only the most clear and extended version of this belief. (Webb spoke of administrative arrangements, rather than of a state.) Most saw the state as transparent, Webb saw it as controllable but was unusual in thinking there was a problem at all. When Tawney identified inequality, the objection was not to the bias this gave to the state, or to the bias of power that was inherent in government, but to the consequences of this inequality for the opportunities of the state's subjects.

In its attitudes towards the general arrangements of government, and its acceptance and respectful valuation of the constitutional arrangements of the United Kingdom, British socialism had always been profoundly deferential to what it saw as constitutional tradition. So respectable has British socialism been in this respect, that it has seldom even produced proposals for sensible, moderate, constitutional reform. The optimism with regard to the state reached its climax at the mid century, when the end of the Second World War and the election of the first majority Labour government seemed to offer the prospect of a people's state. When in 1931 the Labour Party had done particularly badly at the game of office, there were some dismissals of parliamentary government. Harold Laski made gloomy noises about the possibilities of socialists being allowed to achieve anything substantial by parliamentary means. But the same people who were so disenchanted in the 1930s became uncritical advocates of ministerial discretion when Labour took office with a large majority in 1945. 'The real alternative to the House of Commons', Laski then declared, was 'the concentration camp'.[12]

Such doubts as were raised about the reliability or appropriateness of the existing institutions of government were voiced from two directions. On the one hand were those for whom the state was a capitalist state, which needed either treating with great caution, or completely replacing with something more worker-friendly. Doubts about the possibility of achieving socialism under the existing constitution, because that constitution was seen as inherently favourable to the interests of capital, were expressed in the 1930s, withered in the 1940s, and revived again with the flourishing of academic Marxism from the 1960s onwards. But the conclusion drawn in each case was that social democrats needed to be both realistic and resolute. Revolutionary or insurrectionary socialism, though it gained some brief encouragement from the Russian Revolution of 1917, has never been a significant part of socialist thinking in the United Kingdom, and the recommendations of the sceptics were that democrats should not expect too much, rather than that they should storm either Whitehall or the City of London.

On the other hand there has also run within socialism a semi-anarchistic vein, which has been suspicious of government as simply one more form of power, and one not necessarily to be exercised in the interests of those governed. Without being individualistic, this strand from Morris through to various forms of workers' control, has stressed communal self-management, both in production and in the management of public life. But whilst it led to proposals for decentralising the control of paid work, it had less to say about dispersing the powers of government.

The mainstream of British socialism has been social democratic. It has sought to extend democracy by achieving one adult one vote, and to extend the power of democracy by increasing the powers of the representative state. At the same time it was assumed that public ownership and social services, by raising the standard of life and hence the capacity for political participation of ordinary people, would enable the fullest use to be made of democratic citizenship.

The response of Beatrice and Sidney Webb to guild socialism at the beginning of the twentieth century was representative. Democracy was a system where citizens in their most universal role, that of consumers, collectively made decisions for society as a whole. To allow such powers to less comprehensive groups, particularly in their most familiar and most sectional form of producers, was to permit not an extension of democracy but a restraint upon it. In this version of socialism, pluralist democratic politics has been viewed with some of the suspicion which attached to self-interest and the exploitation of property, and fraternity has been reinterpreted to mean solidarity.

In consequence of their friendly attitude towards the state, socialists have tended to have little to say about its reformation, and little original to contribute to the discussion of the appropriate character of political activity. Apart from a general sympathy towards the creation of full adult suffrage and the abolition of electoral privileges, it was not until the 1980s that socialists began to adopt proposals which had in the past been associated with liberalism: open government, electoral reform, and a renewed stress on civil liberties against government. This arose from a conservatism towards the constitution, and optimism of a limited kind about human nature, particularly the human nature of politicians, managers and administrators. Under socialism, politics would be transformed from within, and would be played out by socialist man. With this transformed, or at least improved, version of humanity, the alteration of mere institutions would not be relevant or particularly useful or helpful. If those institutions were at the same time regarded as both the best in the world, and as the proper inheritance of the aspiring working class, then there could be little question of their radical reformation.

VI Trailer

If workers could, as producers, be capitalists – and that was the implication of arguments about workers' control – why could they not exercise similar rights as consumers? That, after all, was where democracy counted, and where it was rooted in the universality and commonalty of consumer needs. Socialism, by the beginning of the last quarter of the twentieth century, had reached an impasse in attempting to decide precisely what the society was from which it began its arguments, and precisely what was involved in speaking in social, rather than individual, terms. The renewed debates over both property and markets were to provide a possible way out and forward.

But at the same time the debate over markets was to develop within one of socialism's most profound paradoxes: on the one hand, the assertion of the social contribution and claim to production, on the other the assertion of the rights of workers. The latter could lead in the direction of either class autocracy or property and markets.

In one curious way, the legacy of George Orwell was put to good use by market socialists. He had argued that socialism should be based on the existing character, rather than the potential achievement, of the ordinary people of Britain. Market socialism was to make a similar claim, though without any uniform expectation of what, in such circumstances, ordinary people would choose.

5

FEMINISM

I Introduction

When the novelist Rebecca West said that she did not know
what feminism was, but men always accused her of it whenever
she refused to behave as a doormat, she was making more than a
political joke. The difficulty in saying exactly what feminism is
has arisen in part because though feminism has affinities with
many of the other strands within political thought, it has not
fitted readily into any of the existing categorisations or descriptive themes. In the graphs whose axes are set by individualism
and collectivism, or tradition and innovation, or markets and
politics, there seems no appropriate place in which to place
feminism. It has at various times had associations, more or less
strong, with the other themes in British political thought. But it
has always involved distinctive insights, and has over time contributed as much to them as they to it. Feminism has presented a
challenge of the most fundamental kind to the 'actually existing'
versions of all of the other principal traditions of political argument. It has done so in two ways. First it has advanced the
notion of patriarchy – systematic power and exploitation exercised on lines of gender by men over women. Second it has
widened, or perhaps reorientated, the concept of politics. Both
socialism and liberalism had worked with a conception of the
public space which excluded much that feminists would regard
as of fundamental importance. Feminism, uniquely, has always

85

been concerned with the public and the private, and with both the actual and the ideal relationship between them. Feminism has necessarily and very specifically denied the distinction between a public world and a private world which has been central to liberalism and, in a slightly different way, of great support to conservatism. But it is conservatism which comes closest to feminism in that respect, in that it too regards 'private', 'domestic' and 'personal' affairs as of the utmost importance. But whereas for the conservative they form part of the living and traditionally rooted body of society which government must respect and sustain, but not seek to judge or amend, for feminists they form the root of patriarchy where it is the task of feminists to dig, and to dig politically, the most deeply.

Feminism, as opposed to the isolated indictment of sexual inequality or oppression, developed as a response to the inconsistencies of socialism, liberalism and anarchism, and as an attack on the assertions of conservatism. The various versions of equality espoused by the first three failed to take account of the female majority of the population, whilst the confident inequality defended by the latter called forth a criticism of articulate patriarchy.

One further aspect of feminism has distinguished it from other kinds of political thought. Feminism has used active, propagandist political argument. The more an argument involves saying that the emperor has no clothes, the more forms of argument other than the conventionally rational are likely to be employed in attempting to shift the context of discussion by a shock to the experience. This has involved feminism, more even than the anarchism from which the term comes, employing the method of propaganda by the deed.[1] But whereas the anarchist propaganda by the deed was usually a form of tactical violence against the state or some figure symbolic of it, feminist propaganda has not in general been violent, but has involved the use of comedy, ritual or symbolic action to challenge or illuminate by means of shock the perceptions of opponents or of potential supporters. During the suffrage campaign of the Pankhursts' Women's Social and Political Union, the simple fact of women speaking and persisting in speaking at public meetings was of as much significance as what they actually said. Seventy years later at Greenham Common, the feminist demonstrators against cruise missiles held picnics on the weapon silos and decorated the barbed wire with teddy bears.

Feminism has been more single minded than the other three major strands. It has, in one way or another, been an accusation that women were oppressed, and a demand that that oppression be ended. To that extent it has had a finer cutting edge than the other arguments. But it has been a cutting edge of almost universal application, so that there has been no area of life to which the feminist analysis cannot be applied.

But whilst feminism has been single minded, its arguments have not been uniform. There is no single answer to the question 'what does the ending of the oppression of women involve?' There is no single response to the enquiry as to what a society without such oppression would be like. Feminism differs from other traditions of political thought in that its principal characteristic is an analysis of oppression, rather than a proposal of principles or a defence of existing interests. So whilst there is a variety of arguments about what it would be like to live in a society from which the oppression and exploitation of women by men had been removed, the range is far greater than would be found amongst socialists, conservatives or liberals. It is in the analysis, rather than the prescription, that the coherence of feminism has been found. That analysis centres on the belief that a significant, or the most significant, division of power, status, advantage or opportunity in society is that between men and women.

The relative weight within feminism of analysis over the description of comprehensive alternatives has not, however, been because there has been no feminist speculation at all about alternative futures, or examination of values and institutions different from those which predominate at present. There have been many such investigations and speculations, but they have all had worrying implications for the analysis of gender inequality. A recurring feature of feminist argument, though as much because of historical association as by logical necessity, has been the suggestion that women possess distinctive qualities which in many respects make women, and the character of female groups and institutions, superior to or preferable to men and male groups and institutions. If a projected utopia envisages most existing distinctions as having disappeared, since they are gender based and hence socially constructed, then not only has women's oppression disappeared, but so to an extent have women. If on the other hand a distinctive female character is thought to be inherent, and thus to be found in any hypothesised future society, then it seems that the argument is coming dangerously close to conservative arguments about biologically based differences between the character of the sexes.

Whilst feminist political argument has been distinctive, it has frequently developed in debate with other views, particularly with liberalism and socialism. This is so for two reasons, which are both aspects of the same reason. Liberalism in the nineteenth century and socialism in the twentieth were the bodies of political theory from within which came demands for freedom, the ending of oppression, and the righting of wrongs. To that extent they articulated general principles which feminists could share. But at the same time in the application of those principles liberalism and socialism showed precisely that mixture of blindness to gender and acceptance of its role as a fundamental division of power and advantage which was for feminists the root of the problem. Conservatism was explicitly patriarchal and could simply be opposed. Liberalism and socialism on the other hand appeared to have fundamental flaws running through them which could be leverage points for new departures. If their commitment to liberty and equality were fully thought through, their other commitments would be transformed beyond recognition.

Whilst feminism has used limitations or inconsistencies within bodies of argument such as liberalism or socialism to develop new positions of its own, one widely used rough categorisation employs the terms liberal, radical and socialist to identify the principal feminist viewpoints. Liberal feminists, in this usage, are those who believe in rationality and persuasion, and the possibility of negotiated solutions in the interests of all. Much feminist argument for the extension of the vote to women was of this kind. The deprivations of which women complained were seen as being as much the result of misunderstanding as of deliberate oppression, and could hence be set right by reasoned amendments to existing arrangements. Socialist feminists have developed the idea of economic self-interest to explain sexual inequality as at root a matter of economic power. Hence the beneficiaries from the exploitation of women lack the innocence with which the liberal view can sometimes excuse them. There is disagreement, though, as to whether those beneficiaries are men as a whole, or principally capitalists or the capitalist system. Radical feminists have no such doubts. The oppression of women is the result of a specific structure of power, often termed patriarchy, which is based on sex and which disadvantages women as a group in the interests of men as a group.

II History

Much of the history of feminist thought has been, it is argued, either concealed or distorted. Feminists have frequently been sceptical of suggestions that some particular part of their arguments is novel. It is simply, they retort, that it has previously been overlooked or deliberately set aside. The periodisation of feminism into a political, electoral, legal and constitutional 'first wave' up until the first, partial extension of the parliamentary vote to women in 1918, and an economic, sexual, domestic and ideological 'second wave' from the late 1960s onwards has been similarly criticised. Dale Spender has suggested that this is one more way of obscuring the comprehensive character of early, pre-First World War feminist thinking.[2]

Because feminism has not been a doctrine of government, it has not always responded to political events in the way that the other principal traditions have done, save in so far as those events have been legislation, or the promise or denial of legislation, affecting the position of women. The history of feminism has thus been set more firmly in the context of the uneventful course of gender division, the slow movements of economic and social structures, and the changing patterns of argument and opinion about them. So the industrial revolution which led to the creation of a vast class of propertyless wage earners at the same time pushed women away from independent occupations, or partnership in family economic occupations, and into the career of 'upper servant'.[3] The characteristic movements of industrial society used the language of liberation and emancipation, but singularly failed to include the female majority in their indictments of the industrial order. Feminism has hence acted as a leverage within the inconsistencies of the existing order.

Feminist thought has developed in part in response to the perceived inadequacies of other political arguments at times when they were themselves enjoying apparent success. At the same time, it has frequently pursued the implications of those arguments further than their more conventional advocates, in the course of so doing creating a contribution which is more innovative and more lasting than the ideas in whose company they first seemed to have developed. Mary Wollstonecraft's *A Vindication of the Rights of Woman* was written at a time when radicals like Paine, reflecting on the revolution in France, were speaking of the rights of man. In the nineteenth century arguments for an extension of the parliamentary vote to women accompanied arguments as to why the vote should be extended to wider sections of the male population.

This meant that liberal criticism of the constitution of the citizen electorate was given its most thorough development by writers such as J. S. Mill and, earlier, Wollstonecraft; that the socialist criticism of capitalism was accompanied by a feminist criticism of the economics of marriage; and that the demands for liberty and equality made within the loose alliance of arguments grouped under the title 'New Left' in the 1960s and 1970s, received their most far-reaching development in feminist thinking on domestic relations.

So in the late eighteenth and early nineteenth centuries, feminism had a neighbourly relationship with radicalism, and thereafter and into the twentieth century, with socialism. It developed the implications of the former's doctrine of rights and the latter's doctrine of equality to denounce the denial of rights or equality to women. An argument which attacked fundamental aspects of the established order of things naturally found more congenial associates amongst those who, even if with less sweeping intentions, found themselves similarly at odds with prevailing values and institutions.

There is thus something that is true and something that is misleading in a 'two-wave' and any other combination of waves theory of feminism. Feminist political thought, like any other, has had its history and has been advanced in particular historical circumstances, both political and intellectual. At the same time, much that was treated as novel and outrageous by opponents had been set forward many times in the past.

Three areas of feminist criticism and political attention can certainly be identified. First the electoral, constitutional and legal; second the economics of the public sphere, and the employment conditions and opportunities of women, and of men; and third the household. At different periods, different areas, or combinations of areas, have received the bulk of attention. But this has not been because the household was never the subject of feminist attention before the 1960s, but in part a matter of tactical opportunism, in part a response to the most pressing disadvantages and the most promising opportunities.

The impression of a great increase in the volume and variety of feminist thought from the 1960s onwards is thus partly correct, partly misleading. More was written, and the implications of feminism for a wide range of political, social and historical thought examined more thoroughly than ever before. At the same time the response to feminism, defensive, aggressive, sympathetic and assimilative, was more widespread. But much that seemed novel did not lack precedent, and much that was greeted with outrage by critics had been said or implied in one way or another many times since the publication of Wollstonecraft's *Vindication* in 1792.

Nonetheless a rough chronology can be sketched, and one which follows the general outlines of the 'wave' theory. In the first phase, when feminism drew its own lessons, just as conservatism had done, from the French Revolution, there was both a use of international and even universal frameworks of reference – the rights of womankind – and an address to the specific legal inequalities under which women suffered. A second phase, leading up to the suffrage feminism of the years before the First World War, was more specifically domestic, drawing much of its argument not so much from broad principles as from the inconsistencies of existing arrangements and the justifications advanced in their defence. But at a time when socialism and social democracy was analysing the ways in which economic power qualified formal democratic rights, feminists too looked further than simple constitutional reform. The period of suffrage feminism overlapped with the development of a feminist analysis both of the practices as opposed to the law of employment, and of marriage and the household as economic institutions where women carried their own unique form of work, and made their own onerous contracts. Finally from the 1960s, feminist argument both broadened and diversified. On the one hand it undertook a comprehensive analysis of the entire range of gender inequality – public, private, political and domestic – and of the systematic relations between them. On the other it became part of a wider debate, which though located in this country and having a specifically British dimension, drew on an international body of feminist thinking and writing.

III Society

There had been an assumption shared between conservatives and liberals that society was in some sense distinct from government. They disagreed about how society was to be understood in such a categorisation, where the boundaries ran, and how society was made up. Both conservatives and liberals shared with socialists an assumption that although the family and the household were in one sense part of society, and for both liberals and conservatives, though in different ways, a fundamental social institution, there was a sense in which the household or family occupied a third position which was removed from both state and society. In liberal thought the household was a sphere of privacy and freedom, where the constraints of the public world of politics and the economy were, if not banished, then at least kept at arm's length. But whereas most socialists had nothing to say about the private sphere of the family, and conservatives had both taken it as given and exalted it to near utopian heights as the model of all social virtue, feminists placed it firmly at the centre of their argument about the oppression of women. In so doing they redrew the distinction which had been made, sometimes explicitly, sometimes implicitly, between 'private' and 'public'. The family was the fundamental social institution, and any discussion of society had to begin there.

The 'private' sphere of the household was not the citadel of freedom and security which it was often represented as being. Nor were domestic relations all the result of unconstrained individual choices. Rather, they were the result of regular structures, and as such were no more private than were relations in the paid workplace. As such they were a proper matter for the attention of those who wanted to understand how social relations were sustained, as well as for those who wanted to end the special privileges which systematically advantaged men against women.

Mary Wollstonecraft's analysis of the oppression of women had begun with their condition as 'private' individuals. Olive Schreiner in her 1911 *Woman and Labour* identified the root of the inequality of woman in her unaided responsibility for unpaid domestic labour. Christabel Pankhurst's controversial *The Great Scourge* centred on the position of married women as unpaid performers of a vast range of domestic duties: 'cooking, laundry work, dressmaking, marketing, mending, scrubbing and cleansing, bathing, dressing and general care of infants, housemanagement, sick-nursing, social entertaining, husband's career making', whilst Cicely Hamilton began her analysis *Marriage as a Trade* with the family and the distribution of power within it.[4]

The 'private' sphere of family life was considered important in two principal ways. First, the burdens placed on women in the household handicapped them in their activities outside the home, whilst having the reverse function for men. Second, the institutionalisation of dependent and subordinate femininity in the household was carried over into, or infected, the public space so that in addition to the handicap of their household role, women were treated as a class apart largely on the basis of the values and practices located there. Inequalities formed an inter-locking and self-sustaining system. Whilst for some feminists, the burden of unrewarded production in the home hobbled women in their lives outside the home, for others it was only the system-atically depressed rewards and opportunities available to women in paid employment which forced them into marriage 'as a trade'.[5]

The emphasis on the household as a place of sexually exploita-tive production placed strains on any conventional socialist analysis. In 1966 Juliet Mitchell proposed four components of women's subordination of which two, reproduction and child rearing, were firmly located in the home, one, sexuality, might be presumed to be in general located there, and the last, pro-duction, located there in a way unique to women. By the time these arguments had been developed to book length in 1971, concepts such as patriarchy, and 'male chauvinism', in effect patriotism on partisan behalf of the male sex, had been intro-duced in order to make sense of what could not be adequately explained by the Marxism of the original starting point.[6]

The deliberately paradoxical argument that 'the personal is political' had numerous consequences. One was to make the household an arena of 'political' action, so that attempts to discover and develop new kinds of domestic arrangements could be presented as necessary social experimentation in much the same manner as the various utopian communities of the nine-teenth century. Another, paradoxical, consequence was on occa-sion the turning inside out of the aphorism, so that purely personal activity became a sufficient form of politics, and an argument over the staircleaning rota became an all absorbing and all sufficient assault on patriarchal society. Far from the political invading the personal, in other words, the personal could on occasion wipe out the political.

But a continuing achievement of the feminist refusal to draw an uncrossable frontier between the 'personal' and the 'political' was a series of analyses of the relationships between problems which had been insufficiently understood by being treated in isolation from one another. Virginia Woolf had argued in *Three*

Guineas in 1938 that the treatment of women within families, the concentration of educational resources on young males, the belligerent manners of politics, and the bellicose conduct of international relations, were all of a piece.[7] It was an argument taken up, though in a different context, forty years later by Sheila Rowbotham when she argued that the principles of conduct which had developed within the women's movement provided preferable alternatives for the whole of radical politics.[8]

IV Economy

Just as feminists extended and reformulated the idea of society, so did they that of economy. For socialists, liberals and conservatives, economic activity took place in the 'public' sphere where people worked for wages, salaries, monetary profits and material rewards. Feminists argued that a major part of economic activity consisted of the work of women within the household, which was left out of account in conventional theory because it attracted no rewards of the kind which distinguished economic activity in the public sphere. This had two consequences. If economic matters were of public or political concern, then that major slice of production which took place in 'private' could no longer be ignored. Secondly, if economic activity was the qualification for a say in the 'real' or 'public' world, women were at least as well qualified as anyone else.

It has sometimes been suggested that this identification of the household as a major area both of economic activity and of economic oppression was a distinguishing feature of the 'second wave' of feminism from the 1960s onwards. In fact Mary Wollstonecraft had drawn attention to it in 1792. At the beginning of the twentieth century the economic entrapment of women in households and in marriage was a central point of the presentation of gender inequality in Cicely Hamilton's *Marriage as a Trade* as well as in Christabel Pankhurst's *The Great Scourge*.

The identification of the issue was easier than the formulation of a means of changing things. Hamilton's argument was that marriage for women as an occupation, as opposed to a relationship, would not survive the achievement of equality in paid employment. Others proposed that domestic work be incorporated in the public sphere by being paid. Still others saw the male/female household as so inherently oppressive that its disappearance was a necessary condition of any ending of the oppression of women.

The distinction between liberal, socialist and radical feminism is very clear here. For a liberal feminist, domestic production was not so much a matter of systematic exploitation, as of irrational unfairness. A socialist feminist would seek the root of domestic exploitation in the world of 'public' production, and present it as an aspect of capitalism. A radical feminist would present domestic production as a major form of production in its own right, patriarchy, and one at least as fundamental to social inequalities as capitalism – or as state socialism.

V State and Politics

Although British feminists have had little to say about the state, save to apply to it a reformulated Marxism with gender replacing class, they have had rather more to say about politics, both about the values and virtues which the existing way of going about things excludes, and about the way in which the apparently neutral culture of representative democracy is a male, rather than a sexually neutral, one, in which women are systematically disadvantaged.

British feminism had begun as an attack on the constitutional inequality of women, and on the discrimination against them in the laws governing the franchise. Political power was seen as the root of all other powers, and feminism argued for equal access to it. To begin with, the feminist position on the state was that it was unrepresentative because of its exclusion of women, and that to that extent it was illegitimate. The argument was not necessarily a democratic one, but it associated most readily with democratic calls for a citizen body of all adults. The myopia or deliberate partisanship of government was considered a consequence of male domination, and one which to that extent would not outlast it. All that was of significance about the state, from a feminist position, was that it was in the hands of the male minority. The suffrage argument from Wollstonecraft and Mill onwards assumed that the principal wrongs of sexual inequality would be set right by electoral reform, thus setting women on an equal legislative footing with men. Feminism had less to say about the structure or character of the state until Virginia Woolf in *Three Guineas* argued that male power in politics was of a piece with a wide range of other undesirable and destructive features of human society. Women did not merely want to participate on equal terms with men in a constitutional world which men had made. On the contrary, they could only engage in public life by transforming it, and new forms of law, and government, as of diplomacy and international relations, were a concomitant of any end to patriarchy.

This theme was revived in the 1970s as feminism emerged as one of the most distinctive, lasting and innovative elements within the 'New Left'. Male politics, argued Sheila Rowbotham in 1979 in *Beyond the Fragments*, stressed leadership, conflict, personal charisma, centralised power and mass followers. Female politics, on the other hand, was consensual, collaborative, and distinctly suspicious of individual prominence.

Thus there were two aspects to feminist accounts of the existing methods and manners of government and politics. The first was an argument about either the rights of women or the protection of their interests. The existing arrangements denied women their rights and the means to defend their interests by excluding them from political power. The second argument, however, was about the well-being of society as a whole. This was an argument about the character of politics and government, as well as about the qualifications for participation. Restriction of government and politics to males meant that they were conducted in a particular male way. There would be a universal benefit resulting from the ending of male monopolies, since the methods and manners which women would bring to public and social affairs would be different, and superior.

For some feminists the questions of participation in politics and government and of the character of politics and government had to be set on one side until a more fundamental matter was dealt with: what exactly was to be considered politics or government in the first place. Conservatism, liberalism and socialism all either explicitly or implicitly placed the household within the private sphere, separate from public and political affairs, and for some even a haven from them. If on the other hand the household was the location for systematic inequalities between men and women, if the laws and policies of government could be shown not to be indifferent to those inequalities but to sustain them, then a major area, perhaps the major area, of political power had been left out of account. The personal, in the sense of the private and domestic, was quintessentially political.

The implications of this analysis were neither obvious nor single. On the one hand it could be argued that the principal area for feminist attention was the household, and that its involvement in politics and government having been recognised, conventional politics should be used to bring to an end the domestic basis of gender inequality. But it could also be argued that since the household was the source of inequality, it should also be the primary location for efforts to bring about a transformation. The male dominated apparatus of government and politics was of no use here, and to try to work through it was a diversion of energy. Both state and politics as currently constituted and conducted were irretrievably male, and there was every reason for feminists to have as little to do with them as possible.

There were three principal feminist positions in this debate: reformist or liberal, socialist, and radical. For liberal feminists, constitutional arrangements were the result of human choices, and when rational consideration was applied to those choices, there was no reason why constitutional arrangements should not serve whatever purposes people chose. So reasoned argument could lead to reform, and reform could create a system of government and politics which, in so far as the wrongs of women could be remedied by such methods in the first place, would remedy them.

For socialist feminists, political arrangements had to be understood in the light of the social and economic systems of power in which they operated. Constitutional reform by itself could achieve little. It was not dismissed, but could only be effective if part of a more general transformation.

Radical feminists were deeply sceptical of all existing institutions which, in that they were inherently rather than just accidentally patriarchal, could never be employed to end the oppression of women. One obvious conclusion of such a view was separatism, a gendered equivalent of Sinn Fein. Women's organisations should not become enmeshed in alliances or participation with male organisations or institutions, but should develop their own strategies and build on their own strengths.

VI Trailer

More than any other group, feminists had altered the boundaries of the discussion of property and production. Theirs was, correspondingly, to be the most potentially radical contribution to the renewed debate about these issues in the final quarter of the twentieth century.

6

MARKETS AND PROPERTY: THE ALLOCATION OF GOODS AND SERVICES

I Introduction

Britain entered the final quarter of the twentieth century with a tradition of political argument and ideas which would not have been wholly strange to a conservative, a socialist, or a liberal a hundred years earlier. Even late twentieth century feminism, despite the enormous growth and variety which had characterised it, would not have seemed alien to an Edwardian feminist. This was to change dramatically. By the beginning of the 1990s there had been three major transformations. First, economic liberalism had cast off its moderation, and conservatism a huge slice of its paternalism, and both had become radical and aggressive. Together they formed the uneasy hybrid known as the 'New Right'. Second, socialism had been reconstructed as 'market socialism' in a way far closer to the new liberalism of the start of the century, giving a positive role to both markets and property. Third, political liberalism and socialism moved into even closer alliance in the advocacy of citizenship. The realignments which had their roots in the arguments over collectivism at the end of the nineteenth century, finally came to fruition in the closing years of the twentieth.

II Historical Context of the Change

The immediate occasion for the flourishing of both the New Right and market socialism was the election in 1979 of a Conservative government under the leadership of Margaret Thatcher. But the transformation was not entirely sudden, and the intellectual currents which fed the New Right ran back at least to the liberal and conservative reaction to the Labour election victory in 1945. One of the least novel features of political argument is the frequency with which claims to novelty are made on behalf of ideas which are at best refurbished. By the third quarter of the twentieth century, the prefix 'neo-' was being attached to a broad cluster of political ideas, in the mistaken belief that because they were contemporary they must be without precedent. So that despite the continuity in so many of the major themes of political thought, a casual observer might have thought that everything was utterly original, and that the political arguments of the 1980s and 1990s had begun from scratch around about 1979. Liberals, conservatives and socialists were all to be found claiming that their arguments either were in need of renewal or were actually genuine innovations.

Much of what was presented as novel had in fact a fairly long pedigree. It was F. A. Hayek, described by others as a liberal conservative, and describing himself as a Whig, and who had been attacking collectivism since the 1930s, who played Marx to Margaret Thatcher's Lenin, providing if not the intellectual foundations, then at least the intellectual respectability, for government policy and party rhetoric. The novelty lay not in the intellectual weapons, but in the manner and combination of their use.

Conservative governments after 1979 by a series of radical policies on public ownership, employment, public services, education, health and local government illuminated the potential and the limitations of both conservatism and economic liberalism: conservatism asserted cultural and moral values – it also involved hierarchy and subordination; economic liberalism asserted freedom, but did not provide for its equal distribution. This made almost inevitable a reconsideration among socialists

101

of the implications of a number of their own central values, in particular the various meanings of economic freedom, and the implications of a commitment to them.

The wider setting for the debates which began in earnest in the 1970s was the cul-de-sac in which the public ownership, social service state seemed to have arrived. To economic liberals public services and public ownership had always been wasteful and inefficient. But to many of its supporters as well as to its critics, a welfare state, even when it appeared successful in other respects, seemed to operate in a paternalist way. Power was not given to the people at the point of consumption, whatever might happen at the ballot box. Marxists had for several years believed that they had blown the cover of a system which was, in fact, not a philanthropic or wealth redistributing agency on behalf of the people or the working class, but 'a welfare state for capitalism'. Socialists had pointed out that the most consistently successful beneficiaries of the welfare state were neither the workers nor the poor, but the middle class. It thus became difficult to complain both that the state's provision was unpalatable and even poisonous, and also that it was provided in too small quantities.[1]

A welfare state, if it was not to be financed at the increasing expense of capitalism, depended upon rising productivity and prosperity for its own continued growth. This was not inconsistent with the social services contributing to economic growth, but since the relationship was symbiotic, the health of each partner to it depended to a greater or lesser degree on the health of the other. If industry was held back by the inadequacies of the education system in providing trained personnel, a health service funded out of taxation was held back by the limitations of the industrial and commercial tax base. Faced with slow down and decline in the economy from the beginning of the 1970s, there was a choice between a radical departure from paternalist welfare socialism, or a more cautious but steady reduction in social service expenditure. Labour governments in the mid seventies were toying with the second even before Conservative governments after 1979 moved towards the first.

III Property and Markets

The discussion and the realignments took place in particular over the issues of choice, rights, property, and the distribution of goods and services. Markets, whether 'capitalist', 'social' or 'regulated' became a concept around which the various sides contended like seagulls round a discarded sandwich, and property, for long a shibboleth dividing right and left, began cautiously to be pecked at in even the most revolutionary and anti-capitalist quarters. Each of the four principal political standpoints – conservative, liberal, socialist and feminist – has had things to say about markets and on property. What is immediately evident is that none of these views are simply 'economic'. They are on the contrary informed by all kinds of suppositions about family life, social responsibility, the cultivation of the personality, the quality of the political community, and the liberty of the individual.

This is strikingly so in the case of property. Socialism has always had problems with property because although it approves of the benefits which stem from it, it disapproves of the motives and culture which are associated with its possession. The nineteenth century French anarchist, Pierre Joseph Proudhon, had commented that 'property is theft'. To many socialists it was worse than that, and the offence caused was moral rather than legal. Property was not so much theft, as gluttony, avarice, sloth and lust all rolled into one. Conservatives on the other hand have admired the possession of property as one of the highest forms of human activity in society, whilst denying the possibility or desirability of its universal or equal distribution. For liberals the protection of private property has been one of the principal functions of government. They have, however, differed as to whether the distribution of property should be regulated by the state, and whether it was simply an existing possession to be defended, or a potential benefit for all whose distribution should be actively encouraged or even enforced. Feminists have associated property with possession and exploitation, as have both socialists and liberals. Like liberals too, they have drawn attention to the way in which law and

103

public policy have discriminated in favour of men both in the public space and in the treatment of rights over property or children. Even so liberalism has generally stopped short at the door of the family, and has seen property rights as exercised by families within society rather than within families and amongst the men, women and children who compose them. Feminists have thus been better placed than any others to employ the concept of property within the family on behalf of its female and non-adult members.

Property and rights

The New Right and market socialism both relied on concepts of property. Property is a right, though the point might be put the other way round. All rights are claims to property of one kind or another: land, capital, one's own person, educational services, books, a place of unconstrained worship. But the ways in which the argument can be constructed, like the argument over rights, can differ fundamentally. A conservative or an economic liberal theory of property, like a conservative theory of rights, is that the only real and also the only justifiable rights or property claims are those that actually exist. A socialist, a social liberal, or a feminist can claim, on the contrary, that rights are entitlements, and that the value of property to human life creates a corresponding entitlement to it for all.

The 'new' liberalism

All four currents – conservative, liberal, socialist and feminist – fed into the debate over property. And though they sometimes carried the misleading prefix 'neo-' or 'new', what was far more novel was the new intellectual alignments that were developed. The easiest position from which to argue for individual choice was liberalism. But the kinds of liberalism which were available had changed greatly since the nineteenth century. The comprehensive assertion of individual liberty had fragmented into a series of limited defences, of liberty to own property and to buy and sell, of liberty to determine and apply one's own moral standards, of liberty to engage in untrammelled political activity. The most sophisticated reassertion of liberal economic freedom, in the writings of F. A. Hayek, contained the massive caveat that 'a successful free society will always in a large measure be a tradition-bound society'.[2] True individualism, for Hayek, lay not in placing personal decisions above convention, but in accepting conventions and traditions even though they might seem 'unintelligible and irrational'.[3] When Samuel Brittan argued in 1973 in *Capitalism and the Permissive Society* that such a society was possible only under capitalism, it was in a spirit of almost deliberate provocation. The argument was aimed at the settled convictions of both left and right, goading conservatives with the culturally varied and unpredictable consequences of markets, and teasing socialists with the capitalist foundations of moral and cultural freedoms. And in order to reestablish the unity of liberal principles, some took them to a point more extreme even than Herbert Spencer had been prepared to advance them a hundred years earlier. The reappearance of anarcho-capitalism marked a return to the libertarian policies which had characterised the more eager fringes of the Liberty and Property Defence League at the end of the nineteenth century.

But the mainstream liberal argument within the New Right was firmly founded on a defence of economic liberty from which, in a strange mirror image of Marxism, all other liberties were assumed to flow, and to which all other liberties were considered subordinate. The individual pursuit of self-interest, of 'utility' in a free market, was the only acceptable way for goods and services to be allocated.

'New' conservatism

For conservatives the issue of choice posed difficulties as real as those faced by socialists. The combination of a conservative suspicion of purposive state activity with a tory belief in the need for the state to be partisan, created some curious arguments in areas such as education, where parental power and the encouragement of schools to opt out of local authority control were to be combined with a centrally determined curriculum within which all children must study. Central government was to say, for instance, of what history consisted and when it could be considered to have ended. Rate capping was to be matched by date capping. Parents might have the power to choose between the providers of educational vehicles, and they could have any colour they wanted, so long as it was black. The economic liberal would reply that markets only drive down prices if goods are the same. Whilst property might seem happily to go with markets, the conservative theory of property had often been a deeply ethical one, inconsistent with a materialist or instrumental theory of the kind to be found in market liberalism.

To Tories, the market was an uncertain institution. In so far as it was redolent of individualistic liberalism, they opposed it. There is a problem therefore, of reconciling a conservative respect for property with a tory suspicion of its irresponsible or individualistic use. This problem was faced by Roger Scruton in his vigorous restatement of traditional toryism and his insistence on 'the ascendancy of policy over production'.[4] In the past this had led conservatives to be Keynesians rather than supporters of untrammelled markets, and if property was now to be defended and its free trade advocated, it must be because of the social or political consequences this was expected to produce, not because of some liberal notion of individual rights. Property must for conservatives therefore be justified by its moral and social function, as 'the focus of rights and obligations'.[5] Since it is necessary for the social self-realisation of man, the ability to dispose of it in a free market then follows as a logical consequence.

The intertwining of conservatism and liberalism in the New Right and the central place of the family

Economic liberals and conservatives thus approached property and markets from very different directions. Nonetheless there was an historical complementarity whereby the New Right case ensured that the ideological plate was licked clean, the Jack Sprat of liberalism consuming the lean of markets, whilst the Mrs Sprat of conservatism devoured the inequalities which the market sustained and the divisions of status and gender which are necessary to make their particular version of it work.[6]

In forging the alliance between economic liberalism and political and cultural conservatism, the New Right conception of the family was crucial. 'It is a small step from the institution of marriage to that of private property.'[7] The family is the keystone of the liberal/conservative arch, inducing financial prudence, acquisition, property and investment on the one hand, and authority, tradition, and gender and generation demarcations on the other. The pursuit of individual economic gain is raised to a higher moral plane when it is attached to a commitment to dependants both present and future. Cultural and moral authority, demanded as the necessary condition for bringing children to a point where they can assume the full responsibilities of adulthood, both create a prior cultural order within which responsible choices must then be made, and justify by implication the extension of moral authority from the family to the wider sphere of society as a whole. F. A. Hayek's blend of natural selection, inequality, tradition and hierarchy found a perfect home in the patriarchal family.

IV The New Right

By the middle of the 1980s not only was a government firmly entrenched which was widely thought to be, in some not very specific sense, 'New Right', but the ideas of the New Right were gaining greater and greater prominence as the common sense middle ground of political discussion. Arguments stemming from the 'New Right' moved from the liberal fringe to somewhere near the pragmatic centre. As with all such general terms, 'New Right' seems never to apply to any particular thinker, and whenever a specific body of writing is examined, it seems never quite to fit the category. The New Right, whilst it might have some coherence at the level of party, government and policy, was composed of very different strands of political argument. Nonetheless there were some central characteristic beliefs. The New Right argument was the familiar one that state provision was expensive and inefficient, and ill-suited to respond to varied and changing demands; that the market was the only effective way of allocating goods and resources; that the pursuit by individuals of their own ends was both the only genuine motor of economic progress, and the only possible justification for it. The individual was the best judge of his or her own interests, and therefore markets were the most effective way of registering such interests and distributing resources. As the Conservative politician Enoch Powell had argued in 1968, the market constituted 'a grand, continuous general election' where every purchase effectively registered a preference.[8] The complementary argument was that government was the least well fitted to make decisions about purchase, allocation and distribution, and it could only ever do so by imposing in an essentially arbitrary manner uniform patterns on the huge variety of individual wishes.

The arguments of Milton Friedman and of F. A. Hayek, retailed with vigour through the Institute of Economic Affairs, had in the 1960s been paralleled closer to the centre of the arguments in the writings of Enoch Powell. But whilst an indigenous tradition of liberal suspicion of the state ran from Spencer through Belloc to Hayek, the intellectual catalyst for the new assertion of the toughening disciplines of the market came not from Britain or even from Europe, but from the United States. Orwell had complained that the left got its ideas from Moscow and its cookery from Paris but now, as champagne socialists were matched by caviar liberals, the right got its cuisine from Moscow and its ideas from Chicago. Hayek, though living and working in London when he wrote *The Road to Serfdom* in 1944, and remaining a British citizen, had long since flown westwards, and even if he had not severed his connections with Britain, he had dedicated his 1960 work *The Constitution of Liberty* to 'the unknown civilization that is growing in America' and was now part of a North Atlantic intellectual world which spanned Austria, the United Kingdom and the United States. Friedman and Robert Nozick, on the other hand, were never anything but a pure American influence, the one making the economic argument for markets, the other the moral case for property. A minor theme of the intellectual realignments of the final quarter of the twentieth century was thus the replacement of the left by the right as the principal beneficiary of ideas and doctrines from abroad.

V Markets and Socialism

Although for socialists the intellectual campaign of the New Right was initially experienced as wholly hostile, there were in fact lessons to be learnt and even some common ground. The arguments of the New Right involved asserting realities which came to be accepted within socialism, and insisting on values which had always had a place, even if a secondary one, within the socialist tradition.

The radicalism of the break within socialist thought was far more severe than that of earlier attempts to come to some kind of accommodation with capitalism. Those so-called 'revisionisms' had often consisted of saying that, though productive wealth and economic choices were still in private or non-state corporate hands, nonetheless this was no longer capitalism. There was, in other words, a degree of defensive apology about the whole thing. Now, however, there was a positive acceptance and embracing of the very processes which previously had been identified as the root of moral and economic disorder.

Market socialism was developed in a way which involved major shifts of emphasis, and in response to major changes in historical circumstances. First, it was finally conceded not only that the working class was not a revolutionary force, but that it was one which valued and had an investment in individualistic and familial ownership and consumption. Second, it was acknowledged that there was a genuine popular resentment of paternalism in the provision of services which Richard Hoggart had identified in the 1950s as part of a suspicion of a universalised 'them'.[9] Third, the seeds of anarchism and decentralisation sown in the days of the New Left grew, when they achieved the solidity of policy, into something at least as close to the notion of individualised choice as it was to that of collective provision. Fourth, though this fact came into play late in the development

109

of the debate, the renunciation of communism in eastern Europe from 1989 made arguments about the appropriateness of socialist collectivism much more difficult but also much more realistic. So long as 'actually existing socialism' was there with all its many warts, the right could content itself with pointing to the dire warnings in the East, without seriously engaging with the nature of socialism in democratic societies at all. The left, on the other hand, could answer all such charges, and many others about the deficiencies of socialism, by saying that they were features only of the perverted form of socialism in the East. Eastern Europe acted as a filter for the ideological debates of the West, creating a cordon sanitaire beyond which it was difficult for serious discussion to penetrate. The events of the late 1980s changed that, and made the demonisation of socialism far less plausible. At the same time, socialists had to argue rather more seriously than they had done before for the merits of their proposals, and for the proper distribution of functions between socialist and individualist methods of choice and consumption. Large numbers of people, many of them indisputably workers, had in eastern Europe, without necessarily wholly rejecting the former, expressed clear desires for large quantities of the latter.

The changes taking place within socialism were as remarkable as those which produced the New Right. The adoption by socialists of the mechanisms of the market was the single most radical break in the entire socialist tradition. It was not simply a choice of allocative mechanism, or a mere technical choice concerned simply with means. It involved the rejection of one of the most fundamental moral and psychological foundations of socialism, the belief in the superiority of communal motivation or altruism over self-interest, and the possibility of constructing a social order founded on this superior choice. Socialists will have problems with the use of markets because what markets do is to place an item price on everything, and to allocate that price to a particular 'seller'. This is the very contrary of the socialist assumption that the inputs to and rewards from production cannnot be individually allocated, because they are social. The market socialist, on the other hand, sees collective provision solely as a means of facilitating individual choices, about which the individual is the best judge. She is, too, possessed of a 'mistrust of the intentions of bureaucrats and the effectiveness of public intervention'[10] as great as that of any guild socialist. What this meant was that whilst a social dimension in the production of goods and services was acknowledged, there also operated what in other quarters had become known as the principle of subsidiarity. The only justification for providing a service centrally, collectively, or from a higher level in an organisational or state hierarchy, was if it could not be provided locally, individually, or at a lower level. Thus the onus was now on those who wanted to provide goods and services other than in response to varied and unpredictable free choice, to show why they could not be so provided.

Markets and equality

The greater awareness in Britain of the politics and existence of other European nations involved many revisions of the ideological map. This was especially so with the abdication of state socialist regimes in eastern Europe, and the subsequent emergence of a variety of political movements including several on the extreme and militant right. The removal of the 'soviet menace' makes far more difficult the presentation of social democracy as revolution in disguise or to say, as Margaret Thatcher said of the Labour leader Neil Kinnock in the autumn of 1990, 'he is associalist – a crypto-communist'.

If the slow moves in eastern Europe and the climax of 1989 put 'actually existing' socialism off the agenda, a similar disqualification was occurring with the simple, or radical, liberal market. By the following year the market was running into problems in the United Kingdom in health, education and industrial production itself. And if it was necessary seriously to set out what socialism was about since it was no longer adequate to say that it was *not* like eastern Europe, then one of the things that it was about, was equality. Equality had the advantage over another familiar image of socialism, public ownership, that it was a principle rather than an increasingly unfashionable form of government control. It was clear what socialists now thought

111

of the apparatus and personnel of the state. They shared the same kind of suspicion which had informed utilitarianism over a century and a half earlier. It was less clear what they thought of the traditional, if imprecise, socialist goal of equality. Was it to be a condition which enabled all to pursue their own ends, or was it to be the end to which political action should be directed?

Equality had normally been presented, by both friends and opponents, as the antithesis of markets. Liberal critics had argued that equality meant the imposition of rigid uniformities of income, education and health provision, and general well-being by a paternalist state. The response to this charge had its roots as much in political liberalism as in socialism. 'New liberals' such as Hobhouse had argued at the beginning of the century that equality was not so much a thing in itself, as a principle to guide the distribution of other benefits. One of the most important of these was liberty. J. A. Hobson, in parallel, had argued that an initial increase in collective provision of services by the state and even of public ownership, could be the basis for a steady increase in the relative amount of production and consumption which was the result of individual initiative rather than public policy. Hobson's argument that the collective economic activity of the state would decline as a proportion of the economic activity of the whole society, because even though it might grow absolutely, it would enable individuals and small groups to expand fruitfully beyond the basic framework which it provided, provides a precursor to David Miller's argument in 1989 that market socialism does not imply a steadily expanding amount of collective provision.[11]

The development of 'market socialism' involved a confronting by socialists for the first time of the problem and fact of property. Because property had always carried the implied silent qualification of 'private', it had held much the same place in socialist thought and feeling as had sin in the Christian Church. It was clearly to be avoided, but it was also better if it was not discussed. There has always been a strong puritan streak in British socialism, suspicious not so much of sensual delights as of material possessions. Coupled with a class vision of society and politics, this gave a double edge to denunciations of inequality.

The rich had an unfair portion of the world's goods – and it was bad for them. But an acceptance of property was involved with an acceptance of the market. To argue that people should have rights in their use, or non-use, of goods and services, was to give them a form of property right, whether or not those rights were exercised through the use of vouchers or money. Property was implied by equality, for if all were to be equal in terms of economic *power*, the power of property ownership was the first that had to be exercised on egalitarian principles.

Once the right to property was positively accepted, so too was the individuality of ends. Socialism, for all the criticism that had been aimed at it in the 1950s by critics like Crosland that it mistook means for ends, was about ends. It involved a notion of a particular kind of society, characterised by fraternity, and the enjoyment of common services and pleasures. But markets, however much they were regulated, could never be about anything but means. If they were manipulated to such an extent that their outcomes were uniform and predictable, they were not markets at all. So market socialism involved stressing a liberal indifference to substantial outcomes so long as initial opportunities were predictable, as against a socialist concern, akin to a tory one, with the creation of a particular kind of society. Markets became necessary to socialism, and socialism a pre-condition of effective markets.

Work, skills and jobs

The idea of property is not one whose movements can readily be constrained. Socialists had often in the past argued that on those occasions such as the First World War when labour was conscripted, so too should capital be. The contrary argument was that if property rights were to be identified and applauded in material capital, so too should they be in human skills and occupations. Such arguments looked back to Tawney's and the guild socialists' ideas of function and workers' control, and over the channel to continental European ideas of worker participation and joint determination. The worker enjoyed property rights in her job. The arguments for market socialism thus included an advocacy of industrial self-management, workers' control or workers' co-operatives.[12]

VI Feminism, Property and the Family

The family occupied a pivotal place in the 'New Right' argument, since it linked property and culture. For other users of the theory of markets its place was less clear. A liberal theory of consumer choice ought logically to deal with individuals rather than with households, and feminists were rightly suspicious of theories of choice which saw the smallest social units as households. Anarcho-capitalists or libertarians argued for a degree of moral individualism which supporters of the family as a moral institution saw as directly subversive. The responsibilities of women in households depend either upon not extending the concept of property to one's own person and its labour power when that labour power is not remunerated by wage or salary, or treating the labour power of women as 'donated' under special circumstances which allow it thereafter to be left out of account. So some feminists have argued that household production ought to be treated like any other form of work, and remunerated as such. They took economic liberals at their word, and demanded wages for housework.

There was a further step in the employment of the concept of property against conservative paternalism. Property was a right, albeit of a conservative kind. And the most basic form of such a right was over one's own person. So in feminist argument the concern for property rights in capital was paralleled by demands for personal autonomy in sexual and domestic relationships. The right to property, which seemed quintessentially liberal, became a Trojan horse for crossing the frontier between the private and the public.

Advocates of market socialism such as David Miller have argued that the concerns of feminists are distinct from those dealt with by their own arguments.[13] But that depends upon the definition assumed of economy and of production. The household is excluded in the thinking both of orthodox capitalist and socialist writers. It is not clear what the consequences for debates about property would be of the inclusion of unpaid domestic production within the definition of economic activity. But it is unlikely that they would be small. If property rights are held not just by families or by fathers and husbands on behalf of families, but by individual members within the family, then a great wedge is driven into the unity of patriarchal economic power. The extension of the notion of property to women's ownership of themselves has devastating consequences for conservative notions of patriarchal authority.

The feminist assertion of full personality for all adults caused problems for both liberals and conservatives, the one because they did not want public regulation of the private domestic sphere, the other because they did but not for the ends supported by feminists. The argument became most complex over abortion. For a liberal, 'women's right to choose' might be denied because of the equal rights of the child; for the conservative, it might be denied because the idea of women's rights was subversive of male authority or the duty of motherhood.

VII Conclusion

Property was an idea with radical possibilities for the left, and unwelcome ones for the right, as had always been implicit in Marx's use of the labour theory of value. Moreover, for economic liberals, the transfer of functions from state to market meant shifting the emphasis onto people's role as individual consumers. But the other aspect of their individuality, to which the tradition of political liberalism powerfully contributed, was their role as individual citizens. The watertight doors between one aspect of individuality and another cannot easily survive the translation beyond the intellectually virus-free environment of the seminar or the think tank, and once the idea of individual empowerment is abroad, it is not readily either controlled or contained.

7

CITIZENS, SOVEREIGNTY, THE PEOPLE AND THE NATION

I Introduction

Any discussion of politics will quite soon raise the question of who is entitled to take part. This is particularly so in a democracy where there is a constant interplay between a presumption of universal political participation, and a variety of beliefs about capability, adulthood, nationality and 'normality'. It is assumed that all citizens may participate in the public life of their communities. But who is a citizen, and what are the qualifications for being one? The question of identity is fundamental. But it is not simply as politically active citizens that people are identified. There are two facets to the political identities of adult members of a democracy: one as citizens, the other as subjects. As citizens they are political actors, taking part in the selection, critical scrutiny, and pressuring of representatives and rulers. As subjects, they are the object of governmental action, action which presupposes on the one hand and creates and cultivates on the other a categorisation of them by government as employed or unemployed, English or Scots, male or female, adults or minors. As citizens, people are actively in command of their own affairs, or at least are actively participating in the discussion and formation of policies and the choice of rulers. As subjects they are contributors to the state and to the enterprises which it chooses. Those enterprises may be 'the common good' or 'the welfare of the people' but they are chosen by government, and represent its perceptions, not those of the people. Political identity is formed in this interplay between government and politics, between the received and asserted self-definitions of citizens, and the cultivated or created identities employed by government.

The attempt to define, defend or amend political identity is central to political thought. In the last decade of the twentieth century, this argument has dealt with political rights, statuses and constitutions, and has developed as the rhetoric and politics of class and economic arrangements receded, making way for the essential relations of rulers and ruled, or in another view, revealing their persistence.

The end of the cold war was one reason for this. Another was the shifting context within which people were ruled, both from within the United Kingdom and from the developing institutions of the European Community. Within Britain after 1979 'rolling back the frontiers of the state', combined with centralising powers, raised questions about political liberties which more customary ways of governing had allowed to remain dormant. In relation to Europe, it was easy to see grants and instructions to farmers or to local authorities from the European Commission as contractual matters, without any of the normal aura of governmental authority. New kinds of governing relationship, and the contrast between old kinds and new kinds, threw into relief the political structure of rule, and the functions, advantages and disadvantages of constitutions and contracts.

The status of citizen does itself involve differentiation, not within the citizen body but between citizens and non-citizens. The differentiations of citizenship operate by exclusion and exception. The usual form of such exception is to take it for granted that those who are citizens are 'ordinary people', and those who are not are in some way incomplete, special, marginal or inadequate. Thus minors are not full citizens because they are considered insufficiently prepared, even though the definition of who is a child or a juvenile is an historically shifting one. And so powerfully can this sense of an exclusive group, even a minority, as 'normal' operate, that large sections of the population can be simply dismissed from view. As John Stuart Mill pointed out in

1869, the exclusion from parliamentary politics of women by men was 'not felt to jar with modern civilization, any more than domestic slavery among the Greeks jarred with their notion of themselves as a free people'.[1]

Another kind of relationship has been suggested by economic liberals in the 1980s and early 1990s: between the state as a provider of services, and ordinary people as 'customers' or 'consumers'. But the relationship between customer and grocer is not a political relationship, even if the grocer is prime minister. Such dealings arise not out of a desire to reform the relationship between peoples and governments, but out of a wish to remove some functions from politics and government altogether, and to transfer them to the unpredictable choices of the market. The arguments of the New Right for 'rolling back' the frontiers of the state, at least in the provision of services and the management of the economy, were an attempt to alter the manner in which people thought about some of the major social relationships in which they were involved: those where they got a living and secured their material well-being. Privatisation was also depoliticisation.

In forming the identities of both subjects and citizens, there are two principal sources, one the customs, practices and aspirations of society and the groups of which people are members; the other the actions and policies of government. The question of who we are can be answered either in terms of the relationship in which we stand to government and the state, or in terms of the relationship in which we stand to some other group or category whether of race, religion, nation, class or gender.

It is frequently argued that as citizens people are all equal – their other identities are relevant for their social, economic or religious lives, but as citizens they are neither men nor women, workers nor managers. But whilst the demand for citizenship is certainly a demand for political equality, arguments about citizenship refer necessarily to the qualities people bring to political activity from their other identities or roles. It is what people are before they are citizens, in other words, which is thought to qualify them as citizens. Thus the exclusion of the majority of the adult population from the franchise until 1918 was justified on the grounds that, being women, they could not be full citizens since there were inherent psychological differences between the sexes. The exclusion of the majority of adult males in the nineteenth century was justified on the grounds that responsible citizenship presupposed having an economic stake in the country other than that of simply working and producing in it.

II The Significance of 1979–92

The history of citizenship and of the arguments and discussions about it is a history of claims and counter claims about the qualifications for full political participation. And since those qualifications consist of the various characteristics which people were deemed to bring to their political life, the argument was about the nature and consequences of identities defined in terms of economic status, religious affiliation, national origin and sex. The extension of the vote had involved the slow discarding of disqualifications based on religion, on destitution – to be in receipt of poor relief was to fall into the category of pauper, involving a withdrawal of a range of rights – on insufficient capital, and on sex. By the final establishment of one person one vote with the abolition of plural voting in 1948, the only people who were not, for purposes of electoral citizenship, persons, were children, convicted criminals, certified lunatics, and members of the House of Lords.

The 1980s saw a transformation of the debate over citizenship. Three political developments set the context for this change. First, a Conservative government which, whilst liberal in its economic policies, was aggressively tory in its social, political and cultural ones. Second, the increasing involvement of the United Kingdom in the European Community, with major consequences for the law governing the rights and powers of both government and subjects. Third, the abdication and collapse of state socialist autocracies in eastern Europe, and the consequent untangling of issues of political freedom, government secrecy, internal espionage, and methods of economic manage-

119

ment which the polarisation into free West and unfree East had tangled together into two single knots.

The Conservative government

The conservatism of the New Right had been vigorously insistent on cultural values. People's social identity was not something they could choose at will, because it was shaped by the society in which they grew up and in which they were formed. Nor should government adopt an indifferent or neutral attitude in matters of culture. On the contrary, argued Roger Scruton, it should be positively partisan in its cultivation and defence of historically established values and institutions: 'constraints on freedom arise through the law's attempts to embody . . . the fundamental values of the society which it aims to rule.'[2]

The rhetoric of Conservative Party politicians had frequently invoked these assumptions. A new recruit to the Conservative backbenches at the General Election of 1992 wrote of the importance in politics of determining 'the extent to which specific institutions and arrangements embody the deeper traditions and values of our society'.[3] Norman Tebbit with only half-humorous intent had suggested the cricket test of membership of the nation: true Britons would not cheer for Pakistan or the West Indies. In matters of personal conduct, the campaigns of the moral New Right gained legislative expression in Clause 28 of the Conservative government's Local Government Act of 1988 which forbade the use of public funds in conjunction with the presentation of homosexual relationships as 'normal'. As the Conservative MP Jill Knight put it, they were 'protecting children and protecting the family unit'.[4]

The elaboration of cultural and national identity, however, is not something which can ever be one-sided. The more closely national identity is defined, the more clearly are some excluded as marginal, eccentric or alien. The consequence of being so marginalised is unlikely to be ideological forelock tugging, but is likely to be a more vigorous statement of complementary or alternative identities. The more the colouring in of the national character of the United Kingdom suggests that those colours are the red and white of St George, the more the Celtic periphery is encouraged to clothe its own identity in Welsh dragons or Scottish saltires. So what for the New Right was a matter of seeking stricter definitions and greater uniformity of standards, was for others a matter of asserting equalities of rights and differences of culture, of insisting on cultural pluralism against cultural collectivism.

The European Community

The development of a European body of law and a European jurisdiction has meant that people have slowly become subject to different bodies and to different bodies of law for their various social functions and relationships. For the first time since the emergence of the modern state, people have been faced by a choice of masters, or rather by overlapping, plural relationships of government. Were the powers of the European Community to be extended, inhabitants of Great Britain and Northern Ireland would be governed by some institutions for some purposes, others for other purposes. In some cases, this has already presented itself not as functional differentiation, but as the existence of alternative levels of jurisdiction, with a degree of choice on the part of the individual or group as to which jurisdiction is, for them, the more appropriate or advantageous.

Europe offers the possibilities of smaller national units, or aspirant national units, within existing states, loosening the ties that bind these units to their existing national constitutions without departing into a limbo of increasingly small and increasingly powerless statelets. The blurring of the edges of the sovereign state in the United Kingdom by membership of the European Community has facilitated, though it has not caused, the assertion of nationalist arguments by the Irish, the Welsh and the Scots. For Scotland, as possibly even for Northern Ireland, greater autonomy from Westminster combined with greater direct association with Brussels and Strasbourg provides a pragmatic encouragement to nationalism. The demand of the Scottish National Party has been not for simple independence, but for independence within Europe. The presence of the

European framework within which national identity could be asserted meant that the demand for independence was not a demand for isolation.

At the same time, the loosening of frontiers associated with greater European union will have unpredictable consequences on people's sense of themselves, of who is foreign or alien, and what divisions in terms of race, age and gender constitute 'normality'. The dilution of existing national frontiers and the growing ease of movement, habitation and employment within the European Community have meant that in any existing national territory there are citizens of the Community who are not, in the old sense, citizens of the places in which they live or work.

Enthusiasts for the European idea argue that the development of the community is not only the single most important event in European politics in the present century, but has fundamental implications for the way we think about government and politics. It is strange therefore that there is virtually no body of political thought which can in any way be described as 'European'. Europe, as an idea, seems to be visible only by displacement. We can tell it is there by the effect it has on other things – arguments about rights, or constitutions, or sexual equality – rather than by any direct presence of its own. There have been enthusiastic discussions of the reasonableness of European co-operation, and of its likely benefits in living standards, peaceful co-existence, or cultural richness. What has so far not emerged is anything less pragmatic, or more conducted with reference to either general principles of politics and government or general conceptions of political identity.

The collapse of state communism

The collapse of state communist regimes in eastern Europe from the end of the 1980s, a neat celebration of the 200th anniversary of the French Revolution, created an initial presupposition in favour of whatever regimes the newly liberated peoples developed to replace bureaucratic despotism. What very rapidly emerged through the dust of crumbling state structures were self-conscious nations whose frontiers had been ignored or suppressed, particularly within the Union of Soviet Socialist Republics. Nationalism, at least for a while, became once more respectable. But as the Soviet Union creaked apart like an iceberg entering warmer seas, different ways of categorising the contending factions needed to be adopted. The differences between the Communist Party old guard and the reformers were not between left and right, or indeed between right and left, but between those who wanted to concentrate and conceal power, and those who wanted to disperse and reveal it. It was a difference which liberal reformers of the nineteenth century would have recognised, and it was not wholly perverse in these circumstances to talk of the old regime as 'conservative', or to group the opponents of reaction in the East with supporters of constitutional and governmental openness in the West.

Liberals in western Europe had always been critical of the denial of political liberties in the East. Movements such as the Czechoslovakian Charter 77 enabled them to argue a common case for political liberties and open government in both East and West. The dramatic and literal opening up of the archives of the secret state in the East after 1989 supported the demands for equal openness in the West. Conservatives who had been rightly scornful of the argument that liberal freedoms were of secondary importance in communist regimes because greater causes took precedence, now found the argument neatly turned against them when they attempted to defend restrictions on open government and free politics at home.

III Identity: Nationality, Race, Gender

The Britain which was becoming increasingly involved with Europe in the final quarter of the twentieth century was very different from the Britain of the previous half century. Whether characterised as social democratic collectivism or as managed welfare capitalism, Britain had in the half century after the First World War been a society divided, and paradoxically united, principally along lines of socio-economic class. Irish independence in 1922 had removed the possibility of serious religious or nationalist divisions. Britain's government had been collectivist, its politics social democratic. From the end of the 1960s this predominance of class was steadily eroded by a resurgence of the politics of nationality, as well as of race, religion and gender.

Nationalism

Nationalism has been more evident in political organisation and programmes than in political thought. Straightforwardly political writers have tried to give an account of politics within the United Kingdom and of the place of nationalisms in general, rather than an account of any particular national identity. Descriptions and celebrations of this identity are to be found elsewhere, in the work of poets, dramatists and writers. For the Welsh poet Saunders Lewis writing in 1936, culture lay at the root of politics: 'Courage in social economic enterprises depends on a true sense of citizenship, of consciously inheriting from the grave and confidently building for the cradle.'[5] Over half a century later much the same point was being made by the Scottish critic Joyce Macmillan: 'nations define themselves most fully . . . when they are using the stuff of their own language and culture to tackle the substantial issues of their time.'[6] Nationalism is after all not an argument about how political communities should be organised, but about what the political communities are within which politics should take place. Its arguments are even more particular to a certain place and a certain culture than are those of conservatives, and the form which they take even less cast at the level of general political argument. History, description, evocation are its characteristic forms, and its flavour is found as much in the poetry of W. B. Yeats, or Saunders Lewis, or Hugh McDiarmid as in more conventionally political writings. The Abbey Theatre's 1991 production of *The Patriot Game* ends with sentiment and passion, rather than reason, to express the nationalist affirmation.

What is true of the aspirant nationalisms of Ireland, Scotland and Wales is true too of the less obvious nationalism of England. Its voices may be those of George Orwell or Enoch Powell, neither of them poets and both more conventionally political writers. But in both cases, the description of England finds them at their most allusive and lyrical, and at their farthest remove from their usual arguments about the conduct of government and politics. For Orwell, the English identity is 'somehow bound up with solid breakfasts and gloomy Sundays, smoky towns and winding roads', for Powell it is 'the continuous life of a united people in its island home'.[7]

The principal traditions have responded very differently to nationalism. Conservative attitudes have had two aspects. On the one hand, Celtic nationalism within the United Kingdom has been opposed because it threatens the unity of the state. As a doctrine of government, authoritative order and hierarchy, conservatism is instinctively hostile to 'subordinate' nationalisms. On the other hand conservatism has itself been a deeply nationalist set of doctrines, though the nationalism has been English nationalism, presenting itself as a British nationalism for the whole of England, Scotland, Wales and Ireland.

For conservatives, the nation has always been the outer face of an organic society. The identity that held a governed society together also marked it off from other nations with their own identities. This meant that international organisations offended not only by their rationalist pretensions, but by their artificially constructed identities. The more that was claimed on behalf of the institutions of the European Community, the more was in response claimed for a national identity expressed in everything from coinage to cricket.

The socialist response has been varied. Nationalisms within the Empire have been treated both with Fabian condescension as the premature ambitions of the underdeveloped, and sympathetically as the self-assertion of the oppressed. Nationalisms at home have been treated with equal ambivalence. For Tom Nairn nationalisms within the United Kingdom were an assertion of popular power against privilege and reaction.[8] For others nationalism has been regarded with suspicion, as either British/English jingoism, or Tartan Toryism, a regional diversion from the important issues of politics. Celtic nationalism was for Orwell the 'usual power-hunger' and a 'delusion' about the possibility of existence independent of England.[9] The response of

E. J. Hobsbawm to Scottish nationalism in the 1970s was that it simply led to statelets which would be powerless in the face of international capitalism.[10]

For liberals, nationalism has been on the one hand an irrational and bellicose intrusion into peaceful international collaboration, but on the other the justifiable context for democratic development within the United Kingdom. It followed that if a British context were considered inappropriate by those who saw themselves as Scots, or Welsh, or Irish, then constitutional arrangements should reflect this.

Nationalist arguments have posed a double problem for the argument that all adults are equally citizens of a United Kingdom. Democracy has always supposed a cultural community, and thus the argument that minorities in the Celtic fringes should accept the democratic decision of national majorities is rejected for the same reason that Lithuanians and Latvians rejected the claim of numbers advanced on behalf of the government of the Soviet Union in 1990 and 1991. So on the one hand, nationalism disputes the unity of the kingdom, and asserts that the nation within which citizenship should be exercised is a Scottish one, or a Welsh one, or an Irish one, and hence also an English one. On the other hand, however, it implies a condition for citizenship which suggests that problems exist even within a British Isles divided into four kingdoms or states. The nationalist argument usually rests on an assertion of cultural and historic distinctiveness: the Scottish people are a distinct national community, and so their system of government should arise out of this. But if cultural homogeneity is the basis of citizenship, there are other divisions of religion and culture which might jeopardise citizenship in any of the four nations.

Race / ethnicity / religious culture

For economic liberals, communities whose identities are shaped by race, ethnicity or religion have no significance. For political liberals, on the other hand, such groups, like all powerful or potentially powerfully intermediaries between the individual and the state, have been regarded with disquiet. In so far as they represent free individual choices in social matters, they are not of immediate significance; in so far as they constrain individual freedom, they are coercive and undesirable.

For conservatives, the existence of churches, associations and other social institutions has been in principle positively desirable. But in practice conservatives have been highly selective in which intermediate groups they have favoured, and which they have regarded as oppressive or disruptive. Trade unions, alternative faiths, and alternative households have in general been treated with hostility, a hostility justified by the tory conception of the state as the positive custodian of a single national culture. Michael Oakeshott, when he condemned the power of trade unions, used the alienating term 'syndicalism' to locate them firmly at the tinker's entrance to the national household.[11]

A socialist conception of class sees society as divided into groups by occupation and economic power. But the response to class differences has been to hope for their eventual obliteration either with the extension of the privileges of the wealthy to all, or with the growth of a new culture which would be either classless or the expression of working class fraternal culture. Organised employers' groups were by contrast regarded simply as self-interested and hostile to the public interest. But neither in the case of class nor of faction did socialists, with the exception of those who advocated workers' control, envisage a permanent or positive role for groups. Other kinds of communities which were intermediate between individuals and society as a whole have in general simply caused socialists bewilderment. They have lain outside the pale of class analysis and many socialists, like the early Fabians, have simply declared such matters as irrelevant, as irrelevant as cookery or interior decoration. Since religious or ethnic groups have neither possessed nor claimed exclusive territory, they have not been thought to raise a political challenge.

Gender

Whilst it has been possible to dismiss nationalist or ethnic claims as the complaints of minorities, the claims of women have been less easy to dispose of, since they are made on behalf of the majority. A different conception of normal has to be developed, in recognition of the radical upheaval that would be caused if the 'ordinary citizen' were envisaged as female, and maleness rather than femaleness added where necessary as the qualification of the norm.

Although in the business of political organisation and propaganda feminists have stood closer to socialists than to either conservatives or liberals, socialism has had great difficulty in accommodating a conception of society ordered in any significant way along lines of gender. It has at times been just as much characterised as liberalism by the assumption that society and politics stop at the front door of the household, and that the relations of power and status which occur within it are predictable and natural, and at the same time a matter of unconstrained individual choice with which politics has no business. Liberalism, however, both in its political and its economic forms, has involved a more fundamental place for that assumption, and in the second half of the twentieth century, economic liberalism has increasingly been articulated in conjunction with a positive assertion of the naturalness and desirability of gender distinctions.

The conception of the patriarchal family, which formed the central hinge between the economic liberalism and the cultural conservatism of the New Right, led to heightened gender distinction, to men out hunting with their cell phones in the market and women caring for the hearth and the microwave. The liberal strand expects an increase both in self-reliance and self-assertion, and in altruism.[12] But the social, as against the individual, implications of that seem to be that the men will be self-assertive and the women will be altruistic.

The conservative strand in the New Right has argued for a state-led reassertion of the patriarchal household, 'putting Dad back at the head of the table'. Feminism is attacked as both unnatural and subversive. What was needed was to re-establish 'the role of the man, the father'.[13]

128

IV Citizenship

The debate over citizenship which grew with the withering away of the overwhelming simplifications of a politics based on class has revived some older themes. Politics based on class is directed towards the pursuit of the interests of groups and the material well-being of the community. It is a means for achieving ends which are generally unambiguous. Citizenship by contrast emphasises rights of political activity irrespective of the interests which may inform that activity. Turning class politics on its head, it makes material security a means to politics, rather than vice versa. It was possible to give a low priority to citizenship and constitutional arrangements when the interests of all were taken to be, in the last instance, much the same – when the working class were seen simply as those who lacked the privileges of the bourgeoisie. But a view of political identity which acknowledges diversity not just by class, but by gender, ethnicity, religion and nation, needs other means of seeking some workable form of association.

The discussion of citizenship has in many ways been novel. The word citizen has not been a familiar one in Britain. Its use has been more frequent in fiction to indicate that a character is alien, than in political argument to indicate that he has claims on government. 'Citizen Robespierre' signals that we are dealing with a foreigner, just as 'Citizen Smith' indicates that we are dealing with a comic eccentric.

The debate over citizenship is, in the United Kingdom, essentially a twentieth century one. Liberalism, and after the First World War political liberalism, is the tradition which has had most to contribute. The active, rational political life is seen as worthwhile in itself, quite apart from its importance in protecting or furthering the interests of citizens. Liberal citizenship was a rational, contractual concept, a status which enabled thinking and reasoning people to enter into a relationship with government from which they expected to benefit, and which could be assessed by clear criteria.

This political dimension was missing from both socialism and conservatism, in the first case implicitly, in the second explicitly.

For socialists politics and government were a means to economic and social ends. The Fabian socialists had spoken of social democracy as a particular form of politics, where the citizens' power was enhanced by an extension of their responsibility, through the collectivist state, for wider and wider areas of economic and social life. But this social democratic citizenship was instrumental only. Citizenship was to be one more way in which individuals contributed to society. Conservatives, on the other hand, as Quintin Hogg proudly proclaimed at the end of the Second World War, regarded politics as no more than an instrumental necessity, and a fascination with politics as such as at the least odd and at the worst dangerous. This was a position which they were to share, in the twentieth century, with economic liberals. The expectation of salvation, or even betterment, by political means was both a diversion from the true freedoms of the market, and a legitimation for their infringement by government. When Conservative politicians did, briefly, in the late 1980s, recommend the cultivation of 'citizenship', what they envisaged was a kind of 'stout fellow citizenship', a matter not of actively participating in public affairs, but of altruistically taking part in neighbourly schemes of citizens' watch, litter clearance, and shopping for the aged.

The most fundamental appraisal of all these arguments was put forward by feminists, who argued that citizenship, like all other activities outside the household, presupposed the exploitation of women within the household, thus uniquely privileging men and disadvantaging women. Citizenship as active participation in politics was possible for men on much the same terms as it had been in the version described by Aristotle: on the backs of the domestic labour of women which gave men the necessary leisure by relieving them of the burden of domestic production.

In the second half of the twentieth century, liberal arguments over citizenship underwent a fundamental realignment. Political liberalism, which had long since moved in a different direction from economic liberalism, was increasingly articulated in conjunction with socialism. At the same time the feminist critique of traditional liberal arguments on politics added a further dimension to a new radical position on the question of citizenship.

The first stage in this realignment was the account of citizenship set out in 1950 by T. H. Marshall. Marshall argued that there were three stages of citizenship: political, civil and social. The first was a matter of formal rights to participate in politics. The second was a matter of legal securities for free and unhindered economic activity, association and expression in social life. The third was a matter of rights to a minimum condition of life: income, housing, health, education. The significance of this was that it reversed the traditional liberal conception of citizenship which was derived from Aristotle. In the traditional view people were qualified as citizens because of the powers or characteristics which they already possessed. Thus property owners were qualified because they had a stake in the economy, the educated because they were intellectually prepared for citizenship, and men precisely because they were not principally committed to the maintenance of the household. In the new version, the qualifications for citizenship became rights, which society through the state should where necessary meet in order to make possible the fullest citizenship for all adults. What was missing from Marshall's argument was the feminist point that for this full citizenship to be available regardless of sex, the household/family, as a relationship of power and exploitation, would have to be transformed.

Each of the elements of Marshall's argument was developed in the last two decades of the century. Charter 88 and the movement for constitutional reform took up the issues of both political and civil citizenship. It was necessary to subordinate all governing bodies to the rule of law, lest freedom depend upon no more than 'the goodwill of the government and the compassion of bureaucrats'. At the same time citizenship was to be both universal and enjoyed equally by all, and made possible by paying particular attention to 'the rights of women and the place of minorities'.[14] Socialist arguments for a revived theory of citizenship meanwhile reasserted social citizenship in a moderate, and feminist arguments in a radical, manner.

Conservatives have often been indignant at the suggestion that things could or should be otherwise. What we enjoyed here, argued Michael Oakeshott, were not some set of abstract citizen rights, but the liberties of Englishmen. This view, however, came under increasing pressure, not from the arguments of those who advocated citizens' rights, but rather from the less avoidable pressure of historical events. In eastern Europe from the inauguration of the cold war until the abdication of the communist autocracies at the end of the 1980s, liberals of many hues, together with some conservatives, had complained of the absence of political rights, the fundamental rights of citizenship. The upheavals in the course of which those rights began to be taken by the peoples of eastern Europe provided an unsettling example of a criticism turned into a practice.

At the same time, the adequacy at home of the notion of the traditional liberties of Englishmen began to be questioned by those who were able to point out that not all of the inhabitants of the British Isles were English, and that slightly over half of them were not men.

In the European Community a Declaration of Human Rights, a Commission and a Court of Human Rights, and the slow application of some of these rights against the now subordinate judgments of British courts and the practices of British government, presented a glimpse of standards which came closer to ideals of citizenship than did traditional English practices. The idea of citizenship came to acquire attractions, both as a way of securing rule-governed, impartial, government of a society which was neither nationally, ethnically, religiously, nor sexually uniform, and as something which was neither so unfamiliar or so alien as had previously been the case.

But the principal traditions of British political thought had much to contribute to the discussion of citizenship, both to its elaboration and its rejection. One implication of the arguments of the New Right was deeply egalitarian. People had a right to property and to the benefits which their skill or luck or labour could gain from it. No barriers of privilege imposed by the state should stand in the way of those rights, and all were thus equal under the rule of law. Even national frontiers could be shaken by the development of such logic. But there was a conservative strand to the New Right which was just as profoundly hostile to what it saw as abstract egalitarianism. From this vantage point, people received their identity from their history and their society, and neither states nor nations could or should be neutral as between one identity and another. Each state was the custodian of a particular set of institutions which gave the society which it governed its character. In matters of gender, religion, status or ethnicity there were clear hierarchies and clear distinctions of function, responsibility, and duty.

The paradox of citizenship

Supporters of the ideal of citizenship have often viewed it as being rational and egalitarian, and a solution or an alternative to 'irrational' cultural divisions. On the other hand the writer who gave the clearest articulation to the current conception of citizenship, T. H. Marshall, argued that citizenship required its own kind of social 'bond': 'a direct sense of community membership based on loyalty to a civilisation which is a common possession.'[15] If citizenship is viewed as the public, political dimension of a community which is already held together by its social character, then citizenship will also require a degree of shared culture, and will not be compatible with major divisions of identity. Citizenship in this case will be located within the frameworks of nations, religions and identities which are specific and limited. A democracy faces particular legitimacy problems if the state governs distinct communities, problems which are not faced by regimes whose authority is derived not from representation but from, for example, divine sanction. The moment the state identifies itself in cultural, social or ethnic terms, it sets itself apart from those who do not fit this stereotype. And the more substance that is given to this stereotype, the greater the alienation between the state and its 'atypical' communities of citizens. So it may be the case that in the United Kingdom in the 1990s the idea of citizenship has arrived too late, at a time when the country is divided internally, and becoming more so, whilst its common identity is being diluted or qualified at the same time by membership of the European community.

Paradoxically, in recognising and dealing with ethnic or religious minorities, the state might well reinforce these hierarchies, at least within the communities which, by treating them as social entities with traditions, identities and leaders, the state not only recognised but cultivated. Those with whom government deals are not all or any members of those cultures, but individuals who claim not just authority to speak on behalf of those cultures, but authority within them and over their members.

V The Discourse of States and the Discourse of Citizens

Debates over citizenship and the constitution in the last decades of the twentieth century revealed a deep division within political thinking between public discussions and the more restricted discussions of political elites. Since the First World War and the resolution of the conflicts over the powers of the House of Lords, the concept of the constitution has frequently been restricted to what Maurice Cowling has called the world of 'high politics'. Public persons, paradoxically, have worked with a cluster of values and assumptions which are not public at all. This has been not so much a matter of secrecy, but of a discussion in terms of principles which are articulated and understood within a relatively small circle. One of the many novelties of the Charter 88 movement in the 1980s was that it took discussion of the constitution and of constitutional principles into the arena of public debate.

The emerging debate over citizenship provides soil for discussion of the nature of government and the constitution. Since such a discussion had been largely dormant, none of the political traditions had developed their distinctive views or proposals. But liberalism has the most to contribute. Liberalism, although distinguished from conservatism and socialism in its essential suspicion of rulers and its subordination of government to activities which can most appropriately be carried on outside the pale of the state, has been distinguished also by coming closer than either of the other two traditions to sustained critical thinking about the constitution.

Sovereignty

The growth of the European Community has meant the re-emergence of the questions of sovereignty and legitimacy into general political argument. The absence of a written constitution, and the reservation of discussions of constitutionality and sovereignty to lawyers and to constitutional theorists, has in the past kept the topic out of the public domain. It has not appeared with such force since the conservative response to the French Revolution of 1789, when traditional authority had been contrasted with rationalist and revolutionary constitution-making. The debate over democracy had never dug so deep, and the arguments over the House of Lords, though they had had major implications for party politics, had had far less an impact on conceptions of the basis of the state. The proposals of organisations such as Charter 88 are to be explained as much in the light of the constitutional frameworks of the European Community as in that of the protests, before 1989, of eastern European liberals and democrats. Both state and sovereignty have had to be thought about more clearly than in the past, again, paradoxically, at a time when their fit with the actual government and politics of the United Kingdom was less than it had been for four hundred years.

There were two different reactions. On the one hand was xenophobia, the idea of the interfering foreigner or foreign institution, an assertion of the mystical Britishness of things as they are done here. On the other was a sense of the oddity and perversity of British institutions when they come into contrasting conflict with European ones. Conservatism was the most obviously resistant to 'dilution' in Europe, since its doctrine of legitimacy was based principally on tradition rather than either principle or reason. Liberalism, which is suspicious of states and wants to subordinate their actions to rational principles, is less averse to making changes, and more naturally enthusiastic about a rational reordering of functions between several governing institutions. In that the European Community is lacking in any form of legitimacy other than that accruing to the practical instrument of utilitarian policies, and is not grounded in any

135

notion of tradition of nationalist mystery, it is the perfect liberal governmental institution. Government is stripped of its mystification and becomes simply the practical facilitating of the pursuit of the varied interests of those whom it rules. Socialism has grounds for welcoming rationalised and internationalised authority, whilst at the same time being suspicious of any internationalised corporatism which seems to give greater political access to capital.

This process has sometimes been presented as a subversion, erosion or replacement of British sovereignty. That is to misunderstand what is taking place. Sovereignty emerged in the sixteenth and seventeenth centuries as an undisputed monopoly of power within a given territory. When there is a dispersal of power, it is not so much that sovereignty is challenged or usurped, but rather that a post-sovereign form of government emerges. That was the condition of Europe during the Middle Ages. There was no sovereign power, because there were many legitimate dominations: of church, of king, of immediate feudal superior.

In so far as this move from sovereignty to plural domination is simply functional, it does not necessarily increase choice. In so far as it appears to offer a choice of domination or government in respect of the same function, it facilitates the critical appraisal of the alternatives on offer. In the case of citizenship, it can lead to a much fuller debate about the most desirable form that citizenship should take, and of the various legal and constitutional guarantees, surrenders and regulations which may be possible.

This debate, however, is speculative at the moment. There is little evidence that popular attitudes towards Europe in any of the principal member states, or in the UK, involve more than episodic or fragmentary opinions.[16]

If there is an erosion of sovereignty it will involve the increased importance of other, smaller communities. These are not necessarily simply smaller Scottish, Welsh or North English statelets. The relevance of Scotland, or Wales, to the public lives of those who live there would certainly be heightened. But not for all of them, and not for all of their lives. The 'end of sovereignty', if it comes, will not mean the end of legitimate government, but rather its dispersal. People will look more and more to particular agencies for particular functions and relationships, and expect, less and less, that all their demands and expectations can be met by a sovereign state.

A declining adequacy of sovereignty to account for the government of those who lived in the United Kingdom would have major consequences for conceptions of democracy. Democracy grew with the nation state. It involved a clearly identifiable demos from whom, ultimately, sovereignty was derived. The more legitimate domination is exercised by different bodies for different purposes, and on different and overlapping geographical scales for different functions, the less clearly is there a democratic constituency and the less easy it is to construct a democratic politics. This is particularly so with those areas of government which are larger, rather than smaller, than the traditional sovereign state. Much discussion from the 1970s onwards of so-called participatory democracy made a virtue of this diffusion when it involved units smaller than the traditional democratic nations. But when the movement was in the opposite direction, it lacked champions or even analysts.

Citizenship and identity pull in different directions, and can point to either conflict, stasis, fragmentation or subsidiarity. At a time when the very character of government is uncertain, it would be foolish to do any more than point to the many and varied possibilities.

8

CONCLUSION

The present century has seen the transformation of liberalism and the realignment of conservatism and socialism. The last dozen years have seen changes which at close range appear as at least as important, possibly far more so. Yet in judging the consequences of the rise and decline of the 'New Right', of the ending of east European autocracies or of the uncertain fortunes of European unification, there are warnings to be noted. Mao Ze Dong wisely said that it is as yet too early to judge the effects of the French Revolution. Truly massive doses of caution are in that case required when dealing with events of the last half dozen years: the retreat from Keynsianism and welfare; the transformation of eastern Europe; the realignment of political ideas and intellectual loyalties; the 'end of history'; and already the beginnings of the decline of the so recently ascendant 'New Right'.

One consequence of the end of the cold war and the abdication of the eastern European autocracies is the new availability, but not necessarily new clarity, of the terms 'conservative' and 'right wing'. The terms 'left' and 'right' have never possessed academic precision, but their survival has indicated that they perform some important function. After 1989 they began to develop associations and implications which were increasingly freed from the cold war and a simple capitalist/communist, democratic/despotic demonology.

In judging the significance of changes we can only do our best. There is always the possibility that we may have missed the one

thing which to future historians seems of most obvious importance – that we may appear to be in the tradition of Louis XVI
who on the day the Bastille was stormed wrote in his diary,
'Nothing much'. But perhaps he was right about *that* day. The
wisdom of hindsight is, after all, quite artificial and distorts the
reality of the past. There is a great difficulty in attributing
significance. I was writing this book at the time of Maastricht,
but the Danish referendum of 1992 happened before I had
finished it, and subsidiarity took on another meaning. By the
time it was completed, 'post-Thatcherism' was already becoming a familiar phrase to indicate a state of theory rather than a
point in time. It is both enticing and wholly speculative to
extrapolate short term tendencies into long term transformations. But by the time the fully informed and impartial judgments can be made, we will all be a part of the history which is
being assessed.

Notes

1 POLITICAL THOUGHT IN BRITAIN

1. F. J. C. Hearnshaw, *Conservatism in England: An Analytical, Historical, and Political Survey* (London, 1933) p.6.
2. E. P. Thompson, 'An Open Letter to Leszek Kolakowski', in Thompson, *The Poverty of Theory* (London, 1978) p.109.
3. Ibid., p. 106.
4. Peter Baehr, 'Peace "Politics"', *Politics*, 11, 1 (April 1991) 44.
5. James Hinton, *Protests and Visions: Peace Politics in Twentieth Century Britain* (London, 1989) p.ll, quoted Peter Baehr, 'Peace "Politics"', *Politics*, 11, 1 (April 1991) 44.
6. Richard Rorty, *Contingency, Irony, and Solidarity* (1989) p.xvl, quoted John Street, 'Popular Culture = Political Culture? Some Thoughts on Postmodernism's Relevance to Politics', *Politics*, 11, 2 (October 1991) 24.
7. *Culture and Anarchy* (London, 1869, repr. Cambridge, 1960) p.75, quoted W. H. Greenleaf, *The British Political Tradition*, vol 1. (London, 1983) p.29.
8. Ideology is not only a term which is the subject of irreconcilable disagreement – an 'essentially contested concept'; it is also used to refer to two related but distinct concepts. The first is the one I have briefly described here. The other is of a comprehensive, abstract, explanation of human social life, and a comprehensive blueprint for its reconstruction or management. I am not using the term in this second sense.
9. W. H. Greenleaf, *The British Political Tradition*, vol. 1 (London, 1983).

2 CONSERVATISM

1. F. J. C. Hearnshaw, *Conservatism in England: An Analytical, Historical and Political Survey* (London: Macmillan, 1933) p.8.
2. Ted Honderich, *Conservatism* (London, 1990) p.22.
3. Andrew Gamble, *An Introduction to Modern Social and Political Thought* (London, 1981).
4. Albert O. Hirschman, *The Rhetoric of Reaction: Perversity, Futility, Jeopardy* (Cambridge, Mass., 1991).
5. F. J. C. Hearnshaw, *Conservatism in England: An Analytical, Historical and Political Survey* (London, Macmillan, 1933) p.6.
6. Michael Oakeshott, *Rationalism in Politics* (London, 1962).
7. Ibid., p.8.
8. Edmund Burke, *An Appeal from The Old to the New Whigs, in Consequence of Some Late Discussions in Parliament, Relative to the Reflections on the French Revolution*, 2nd edn, 1791, quoted Robert Eccleshall, *English Conservatism Since the Restoration: An Introduction and an Anthology* (London, 1990) p.73.
9. Samuel Taylor Coleridge, *On The Constitution of the Church and State* (London, 1830) quoted R. J. White (ed.), *The Conservative Tradition* (London, 1950) p.101; Thomas Carlyle, *Past and Present* (London, 1843) quoted Anthony Arblaster and Steven Lukes (eds), *The Good Society* (London, 1971) p.137.
10. Walter Bagehot, *The English Constitution* (London, 1963 edn) p.63.
11. Benjamin Disraeli, *Lord George Bentinck; A Political Biography* (London, 1852) p.557, quoted Robert Blake, *Disraeli* (London, 1969) p.282
12. Quintin Hogg, *The Case for Conservatism* (West Drayton, 1947) p.97. Michael Oakeshott, *Rationalism in Politics* (London, 1962) p.51.
13. Quintin Hogg, *The Case for Conservatism* (West Drayton, 1947) p.10.
14. Trade unions had been singled out by Michael Oakeshott in his mid-century defence of conservatism as undesirable coercive bodies, rather than as laudable voluntary associations. Michael Oakeshott, *Rationalism in Politics* (London, 1961).
15. Roger Scruton, *Sexual Desire* (London, 1986).
16. Henry Fielding, *The History of Tom Jones* (London, 1749, reprinted Oxford, 1974) p.127.
17. Enoch Powell, *No Easy Answers* (London, 1973) p.70.
18. Graham Webster-Gardiner, *Crossbow* (Summer 1986) quoted Martin Durham, *Sex and Politics: The Family and Morality in the Thatcher Years* (London, 1991) p.157.

19. Sir Henry Maine, *Popular Government* (London, 1885) p.77.
20. Quoted by Robert Eccleshall, *English Conservatism Since the Restoration* (London, 1990) p.119, from T. E. Kebbel (ed.), *Selected Speeches of the late Right Honourable the Earl of Beaconsfield* (London, 1882) p.488.
21. Harold Begbie ('A Gentleman with a Duster'), *The Conservative Mind* (London, 1924) p.24.
22. J. Enoch Powell, *A Nation Not Afraid*, ed. John Wood (London, 1965) p.28; Sir Keith Joseph, *Stranded on the Middle Ground? Reflections on Circumstances and Policies* (London, 1976) quoted Robert Eccleshall, *English Conservatism Since the Restoration* (London, 1990) p.239.
23. Michael Oakeshott, *Rationalism in Politics* (London, 1962) p.53.

3 LIBERALISM

1. Thomas Paine, *The Rights of Man* (London, 1791, 1792, 1937 edn) p.33
2. Ibid., p.110
3. John Stuart Mill, *On Liberty*, quoted Robert Eccleshall, *British Liberalism* (London, 1986) p.162
4. F. A. Hayek, *The Constitution of Liberty* (London, 1960).
5. T. S. Eliot, *The Idea of a Christian Society* (London, 1939) p.15; Roger Scruton, *The Meaning of Conservatism* (London, 1980).
6. C. B. Macpherson, *The Political Theory of Possessive Individualism* (Oxford, 1962).
7. A. V. Dicey, *Lectures on the Relation Between Law and Public Opinion in England in the Nineteenth Century* (London, 1905).
8. Thomas Paine, *The Rights of Man* (London, 1791, 1792, 1937 edn) p.37.

4 SOCIALISM

1. Robert Blatchford, *Britain for the British* (London, 1902); George Orwell, *The Lion and the Unicorn* (London, 1941); Raymond Williams, *The Long Revolution* (London, 1961).
2. Robert Owen, *Report to the County of Lanark* (1821) pp.20–2, quoted Henry Pelling (ed.), *The Challenge of Socialism* (London: 1954) p.36.

3. George Bernard Shaw (ed.), *Fabian Essays* (London, 1889). Graham Wallas argued that socialism 'appears as the offspring of Individualism, as the outcome of individualist struggle, and as the necessary condition for the approach to the Individualist ideal' (1962 edn) p.138.

4. Sidney and Beatrice Webb, *A Constitution for the Socialist Commonwealth of Great Britain* (London, 1920) p.111.

5. Brian Abel-Smith, 'Whose Welfare State?' in Norman MacKenzie (ed.), *Conviction* (London, 1958) p.67.

6. James Kier Hardie, *From Serfdom to Socialism* (London, 1907) p.86.

7. R. H. Tawney, *The Attack and other papers* (London, 1953) p.165.

8. George Orwell, *The Lion and the Unicorn: Socialism and the English Genius* (London, 1941) reprinted in Sonia Orwell and Ian Angus (eds), *The Collected Essays, Journalism and Letters of George Orwell* (London, 1970) p.78.

9. E. P. Thompson, *Out of Apathy* (London, 1960) p.193.

10. R. H. Tawney, *The Sickness of an Acquisitive Society* (London, 1920).

11. William Morris, 'Useful Work versus Useless Toil' in A. L. Morton (ed.), *Political Writings of William Morris* (London, 1973).

12. Harold J. Laski, *Reflections on the Constitution* (Manchester, 1951) p.9.

5 FEMINISM

1. See e.g. Rodney Barker, 'Dworkin on Civil Disobedience: The Case of Greenham Common', *Political Studies*, 40, 2 (1992).

2. Dale Spender, *There's Always Been a Women's Movement This Century* (London, 1983).

3. Janet Coleman, *Against the State: Studies in Sedition and Rebellion* (London: BBC Books, 1990) p.176.

4. Mary Wollstonecraft, *A Vindication of the Rights of Women* (London, 1792); Olive Schreiner, *Woman and Labour* (London, 1911); Christabel Pankhurst, *The Great Scourge* (London, 1913); Cicely Hamilton, *Marriage as a Trade* (London, 1909).

5. The phrase is Cicely Hamilton's.

6. Juliet Mitchell, 'Women: The Longest Revolution', *New Left Review*, 40 (1966); Juliet Mitchell, *Woman's Estate* (Harmondsworth, 1971).

7. Virginia Woolf, *Three Guineas* (London, 1938).

8. Sheila Rowbotham, 'The Women's Movement and Organizing for Socialism' in Sheila Rowbotham, Lynne Segal and Hilary Wainwright, *Beyond the Fragments* (Manchester, 1979).

6 MARKETS AND PROPERTY

1. The food joke is Woody Allen's. The dilemmas of Marxism are examined in Ian Gough, *The Political Economy of the Welfare State* (London, 1979).
2. F. A. Hayek, *The Constitution of Liberty* (London, 1960) p.61.
3. F. A. Hayek, in Anthony Arblaster and Steven Lukes, *The Good Society* (London, 1971) p.370.
4. Roger Scruton, *The Meaning of Conservatism* (London, 1980) p.79.
5. Ibid., p.99.
6. 'Conservatism provides a set of residual claims to cover the consequences of pursuing liberal policies', Desmond S. King, *The New Right: Politics, Markets and Citizenship* (London, 1987) p.25.
7. Roger Scruton, *Sexual Desire: A Philosophical investigation* (London, 1986) p.360.
8. P. Douglas and J. Enoch Powell, *How Big Should Government Be?* (Washington DC, 1968) p.68
9. Richard Hoggart, *The Uses of Literacy* (London, 1957).
10. Saul Estrin and Julian le Grand, 'Market Socialism' in Estrin and Le Grand (eds), *Market Socialism* (Oxford, 1989) p.1.
11. David Miller, *Market, State and Community: Theoretical Foundations of Market Socialism* (Oxford, 1989).
12. Ibid.
13. Ibid., pp.323–5.

7 CITIZENS, SOVEREIGNTY, THE PEOPLE AND THE NATION

1. John Stuart Mill, *The Subjection of Women* (London, 1869), reprinted in Mill, *Three Essays* (London, 1975) p.434.
2. Roger Scruton, *The Meaning of Conservatism* (London, 1980) p.17.
3. David Willets, *Modern Conservatism* (London, 1992) p.76.
4. *The Independent* (10 March 1988) quoted Martin Durham, *Sex and Politics: The Family and Morality in the Thatcher Years* (London, 1991) p.117.
5. Saunders Lewis, 'Education for Citizenship', *Welsh Nationalist*, 5, 12 December 1936, quoted John Osmond, *Creative Conflict: The Politics of Welsh Devolution* (London, 1978) p.110.
6. Joyce Macmillan, 'Some Notes on Theatre and Nationhood', in Neil Wallace (ed.), *Thoughts and Fragments about Theatres and Nations* (London, 1991) p.10.
7. George Orwell, *The Lion and the Unicorn: Socialism and the English*

Genius in Sonia Orwell and Ian Angus (eds), *The Collected Essays, Journalism and Letters of George Orwell*, vol. 2 (Harmondsworth, 1970) p.76. J. Enoch Powell, *Freedom and Reality* (London, 1969) p.340.

8. Tom Nairn, *The Break-Up of Britain*, 2nd edn (London, 1981).
9. George Orwell, 'Notes on Nationalism' in Sonia Orwell and Ian Angus (eds), *The Collected Essays, Journalism and Letters of George Orwell*, vol. 3 (Harmondsworth, 1970) p.423.
10. Eric Hobsbawm, 'Some Reflections on "The Break-Up of Britain"', *New Left Review* (105 September–October 1977).
11. Michael Oakeshott, *Rationalism in Politics* (London, 1962) p.50.
12. There is a useful discussion in Ian Carter, 'Human Nature and the Utopianism of the New Right', *Politics*, 9, 2 (1989).
13. Graham Webster-Gardiner, Chairman of the Conservative Family Campaign, in Martin Durham, *Sex and Politics: The Family and Politics in the Thatcher Years* (London, 1992) p.156.
14. *Charter 88*, reprinted in Geoff Andrews (ed.), *Citizenship* (London, 1991) p.210.
15. T. H. Marshall, *Citizenship and Social Class* (1950 – London 1992 edn) p.24.
16. As Joseph I.H. Janssen put it in summing up a survey of opinion in Britain, France, Italy and West Germany over the years 1952 to 1988, such support for the community as there was, was 'not based on deep-seated values, well thought-out attitudes, or direct personal experience of European politics'. Joseph I. H. Janssen, 'Post-Materialism, Cognitive Mobilization and Public Support for European Integration', *British Journal of Political Science*, 2, 4 (1991) 468.

Further Reading

The literature on political thought in Britain is extensive. The books listed below represent a very small sample, though many of them contain lengthy bibliographies. Works cited in the Notes have not necessarily been included here, and the selection has been limited in most cases to secondary works, rather than to original contributions to political thought.

GENERAL AND INTRODUCTORY

W. H. Greenleaf, *The British Political Tradition*, vol. 1, *The Rise of Collectivism*, vol. 2, *The Ideological Heritage* (London, 1983) provides the most substantial introduction to the topic. The first volume provides an historical background, the second deals specifically with political thought.

Rodney Barker, *Political Ideas in Modern Britain* (London, 1978) provides a brief if sometimes racy introduction, though it does not deal with the most recent developments.

Raymond Williams, *Culture and Society, 1780–1950* (London, 1958) and Fred Inglis, *Radical Earnestness: English Social Theory 1880–1980* (Oxford, 1982) contain lively discussions of many of the leading ideas and thinkers.

Anthony Arblaster and Steven Lukes, *The Good Society* (London, 1971) contains short extracts from many of the thinkers discussed.

Roger Eatwell and Anthony Wright (eds), *Contemporary Political Ideologies* (London, 1993) is a valuable collection of essays on political ideas in general, rather than specifically within the United Kingdom.

Andrew Vincent, *Modern Political Ideologies* (Oxford, 1992) covers similar ground.

Lionel Tivey and A. W. Wright (eds), *Party Ideology in Britain* (London, 1989) deals with political ideas in relation to parties.

2 CONSERVATISM

N. K. O'Sullivan, *Conservatism* (London, 1976) is a short general introduction to European conservatism.

Martin Durham, *Sex and Politics: The Family and Morality in the Thatcher Years* (London, 1991) is journalistic but informative.

Robert Eccleshall (ed.), *English Conservatism since the Restoration: An Introduction and Anthology* (London, 1990) and

Frank O'Gorman, *British Conservatism: Conservative Thought from Burke to Thatcher* (London, 1986) are both anthologies of conservative thought centred around the Conservative Party, whereas

Roger Scruton (ed.), *Conservative Texts* (London, 1991) deals with a wider – both intellectually and geographically – small 'c' conservatism.

Arthur Aughey, Greta Jones and William Riches, *The Conservative Political Tradition in Britain and The United States* (London, 1992) is a short comparison of two different traditions of conservatism.

3 LIBERALISM

Robert Eccleshall (ed.), *British Liberalism: Liberal thought from the 1640s to the 1980s* (London, 1986) is a useful anthology.

John Gray, *Liberalism* (Milton Keynes, 1986) is a lucid critical essay.

Stefan Collini, *Liberalism and Sociology: L. T. Hobhouse and Political Argument in England 1880–1914* (Cambridge, 1979) is a detailed discussion of a leading 'New Liberal', and New Liberal ideas in general are discussed in

Michael Freeden, *The New Liberalism* (Oxford, 1978).

M. W. Taylor, *Men Versus The State* (Oxford, 1992) discusses the individualist liberalism of Herbert Spencer both historically and in relation to contemporary, late twentieth century debates.

John Gray, *Hayek on Liberty* (Oxford, 1986 edn) is the best book on F. A. Hayek.

4 SOCIALISM

A. W. Wright, *British Socialism: Socialist Theory from the 1880s to the 1960s* (London, 1983) is a useful anthology.

N. Dennis and A. H. Halsey, *English Ethical Socialism: from Thomas More to R. H. Tawney* (Oxford, 1988) discusses the moral strand in British socialism, which is dealt with also in

A. W. Wright, *R. H. Tawney* (Manchester, 1987).

E. P. Thompson, *William Morris: from Romantic to Revolutionary* (2nd edn, 1977) is the best book on Morris.

Bernard Crick, *George Orwell* (London, 1981 edn) is the best book on Orwell.

5 FEMINISM

Terry Lovell (ed.), *British Feminist Thought: A Reader* (Oxford, 1990) is a collection of extracts from contemporary feminist writings.

Juliet Mitchell and Ann Oakley (eds), *What is Feminism?* (Oxford, 1986) is a collection of contemporary essays.

Dale Spender (ed.), *Feminist Theorists: Three Centuries of Women's Intellectual Traditions* (London, 1983) is a collection of essays on feminist thinkers, not all of them British. A wider range of writers is anthologised in

Dale Spender (ed.), *Women of Ideas (and what men have done to them)* (London, 1982).

Les Garner, *Stepping Stones to Women's liberty: Feminist Ideas in the Women's Suffrage Movement 1900–1918* (London, 1984) deals with the social, political and economic theories of early twentieth century feminism.

6 MARKETS AND PROPERTY

G. Cohen, N. Bosanquet, Alan Ryan, Bhikhu Parekh, William Keegan and F. Gress, *The New Right: Image and Reality* (London, 1986) is a series of hostile but informative essays.

D. G. Green, *The New Right: the Counter-Revolution in Political, Economic and Social Thought* (Brighton, 1987) is a sympathetic insider's account.

Kenneth Hoover and Raymond Plant, *Conservative Capitalism in Britain and the United States: a Critical Appraisal* (London, 1988) and

Desmond S. King, *The New Right: Politics, Markets and Citizenship* (London, 1987) are informed, critical accounts.

Julian LeGrand and Saul Estrin (eds), *Market Socialism* (Oxford, 1989) sets out the socialist case for markets.

Ruth Levits (ed.), *The Ideology of the New Right* (Cambridge, 1986) is a collection of hostile essays.

Raymond Plant and Norman Barry, *Citizenship and Rights in Thatcher's Britain: Two Views* (IEA Health and Welfare Unit, Choice in Welfare Series No. 3) (London, 1990) is a debate between an economic liberal and a market socialist.

7 CITIZENS, SOVEREIGNTY, THE PEOPLE AND THE NATION

Geoff Andrews (ed.), *Citizenship* (London, 1991) is a collection of essays on contemporary debates.

Charlotte Aull Davies, *Welsh Nationalism in the Twentieth Century* (London, 1989) presents some of the arguments for Welsh nationalism, as those for Scottish nationalism are presented in

Owen Dudley Edwards (ed.), *A Claim of Right for Scotland* (Edinburgh, 1989).

Index